The
Great
Brain
Robbery

The Great Brain Robbery

Canada's Universities on the Road to Ruin

David J. Bercuson
Robert Bothwell
J.L. Granatstein

McClelland and Stewart

McClelland and Stewart Limited
The Canadian Publishers
25 Hollinger Road
Toronto, Ontario
M4B 3G2

Canadian Cataloguing in Publication Data
Bercuson, David Jay, 1945-
  The great brain robbery

ISBN 0-7710-3514-4

1. Universities and colleges – Canada. 2. Education,
Higher – Canada.   I. Bothwell, Robert, 1944-
II. Granatstein, J. L., 1939-   III. Title.
LA417.5.B47 1)84   378.71   C84-098538-X

Printed and bound in Canada

Contents

CHAPTER I

The Problems of the Universities

Canadians are being robbed. Every year more than $8.5 billion is poured into post-secondary education in this country and every year 163,000 Canadians walk out of the hallowed halls of academe clutching their degrees and diplomas in the hope that somehow they have been prepared for their lives ahead. But higher education in Canada is in deep trouble because undergraduate education has been seriously undermined in the last two decades, and undergraduate education is the core of higher education, the foundation upon which professional and graduate education is built. Put simply and starkly, Canadian universities no longer take only the best students and no longer give their students the best education. The value, if not the very meaning, of a university degree has been steadily eroded.

The university was once a place steeped in mystery for all but a tiny elite. Behind the ivy-covered walls, the upper crust of Canadian society learned gentility and allegiance to the values that underlay the British Empire, made social and business contacts, and in the process picked up a good-quality liberal arts education. Those days are gone forever. Universities became mass education institutions in the 1960s, open to almost everyone, and essential ladders of upward mobility to the sons and daughters of the middle class and, less frequently, of the working class. That was a good and necessary thing. But at the same time, the quality and value of the education being offered declined drastically and that was a harmful and unnecessary occurrence.

It need not have happened. The provincial governments and the universities could have planned their expansion better, and the universities could have refused to become too large too quickly. Standards of admission and standards of grading could have been maintained. The student revolutionaries of the late 1960s could have been dealt with by swift disciplinary action or expulsion. But none of this happened. As a result, the universities of Canada became educational supermarkets, grovelling for government grants, selling their souls in return for public approval and simultaneously selling the value of higher education for a song.

We think the time has come to blow the whistle and cry halt. We have taught at our respective universities for a total of more than thirty-five years, and we have become alarmed and saddened at what is going on around us. We believe very firmly that Canadian universities must do everything possible to regain their souls, and we think that the public will help in this if it knows what is going on and how it is being cheated. All who are connected with the universities are to blame for The Great Brain Robbery. Governments, boards of governors, faculty and their faculty associations, students, and the public all have played their part in undermining a higher education system that, while far from perfect, at least once delivered the education it promised. We who wrote this book are committed to higher education and to the university life, and we fear that this country cannot survive as we would wish it without high-quality universities. That is what we want and, we believe, that is what the public also wants.

This book is a polemic; we admit this at once and

without reservation. We started our teaching careers at the end of the Great Academic Barbecue, the explosion of money and resources that lasted for most of the 1960s, and we have seen higher education eroded ever since. We are angry at what has happened, and we leave the cool, dispassionate analysis to others. We have sat and watched the growth of budgeting systems and administrative and faculty structures that undermined the honesty and integrity of university budgeting and eroded the quality of academic programs. We have witnessed, and played substantial parts in, the spread of collective bargaining and faculty unionization, and we can see the dangers that unionization is posing to the proper functioning of the universities. We are angry at the way governments a few years ago force-fed money into the universities, causing them to run at overheated speed, only to pull back abruptly on the reins with massive effects on faculty and student morale, on overcrowding, and on the quality of education. And we have witnessed the impact of the supermarket style of curriculum that has become almost universal for first-year undergraduates and that allows – and forces – the uneducated to select their own personal route to knowledge, a simply impossible task.

The time has come to reform, and we have written this book in the cause of reform. Unless the real extent of the malaise is revealed, no treatment will be possible. And without treatment, matters will simply worsen further and The Great Brain Robbery will go on unchecked. At bottom, the students and society as a whole are suffering. We believe that it is in every Canadian's interest to see that the erosion of higher education is checked, reform initiated, and the universities restored to a condition of health.

This book omits much. It is devoted almost exclusively to an examination of the structures of universities, to government funding and waste, to the impact of democratization and collective bargaining on the universities, and to the processes of undergraduate education. We have not discussed professional or graduate education to any real extent. It is not that these areas are perfect; far from it. It is simply that our experience as university teachers has led us inexorably to the view that the greatest problems lie in the undergraduate area. And it is precisely there that the foundations for advanced education are laid. If undergraduate education has become weakened, as we know it has, then the entire structure of advanced education is in trouble.

This book will make many people uncomfortable, not least our colleagues and the governments that fund our universities. It will make many people as angry at us as we are at the university system. But we are convinced that the system needs a jolt, an electric shock that might actually restore the heartbeat of the university to a normal pace and rhythm. All we want is for Canadian universities to give a good education, and we invite all those who agree that this a worthy goal to let their governments – and their universities – know how they feel.

CHAPTER II

The Funding Game

The roots of today's university dilemma lie in a region quite remote from the daily squabbles that enliven Canadian campuses. They derive from the historical fact that Canadian living standards rose rapidly in the decades after 1945. Canadians earned more money, in the aggregate and per capita, than they ever had before. As a partial consequence, they produced more children than ever before and for their children they wanted a better life than they had had for themselves. The better life could be defined in terms of consumer products, or sprawling suburbs, or superhighways between the suburbs. It could, and did, mean that luxuries once available only to the Canadian elite might now be made available to larger and larger numbers of ordinary citizens. Among those luxuries was a university education, for in the 1940s only 6 per cent of Canadians leaving the second grade in elementary school could expect to leave university clutching the appropriate sheet of sheepskin; in some provinces today, by contrast, more than 50 per cent go on to post-secondary education.

Procreation and Prosperity

The decades after 1945 contributed something else to education. In the post-war years Canadians were secure in regarding exposure to a university education as something timeless: that is, a classically defined body of knowledge should be allowed to waft under the noses and over the heads of Canada's undergraduate students whether they liked it or not. If they did not like it, they could spend their years on campus acquiring, if not social poise, at least social experience in fraternities and sororities. If they liked it a lot, then they could stay in or around the education system, as spear-carriers in the high schools teaching others to follow along in their footsteps or as galley-slaves in the universities. If they chose or were chosen for the latter, then the rewards included enviably long vacations from early May to late September, a tweed suit, appropriately moth-eaten, a library card with indefinite loan privileges, and the company of other similar beings. It was, of course, always true that the faculty members paid for these privileges through low salaries.

Professors helped subsidize universities because of their low pay; underpaying the staff was a universally popular means of creative and invisible finance for the boards of governors and accountants who oversaw Canada's university system. The French-language universities were even better off, for they had monks and nuns who needed to be paid even less. Everybody, it seemed, was happy. Enough veterans had entered university life in 1945 to keep the colleges staffed, and they helped change the pre-war image of the bewhiskered, tyrannical, elderly, and befuddled professor (who lived in a mode either British – "Gad, sir" – or Germanic – "Mein Gott") into that of the friendly "prof" who could be, and was, played in college romances by Ronald Reagan. The "prof" beamed over his male undergraduates and sometimes played football with them; if unmarried, he would court desirable young females and then settle down to the serious business of procreation. He probably would not know that he was getting less in salary in real terms than his predecessors before the Great Depression of the 1930s.

It all cost so remarkably little. In 1954 there were just under 70,000 full-time students in Canadian universities. Collectively the universities spent $76 million just to keep going and accounted for an additional $12 million in capital costs. In the late 1950s universities were estimated to cost 1.2 per cent of Canada's public service expenditures, compared to 1.6 per cent in the depth of the Great Depression – further evidence of the frugality with which the system was managed.

Of course, many professors eventually went to greener pastures across the border as commentators occasionally lamented what was called "the brain drain." Some faculty members and university administrators worried about it, and some even decried the waste of a valuable national resource. It was, after all, a time of international crisis. National strength was measured in terms of technological advancement. Brains counted in a world where it took a modicum of intelligence to start a nuclear reaction, build a better mousetrap, or even design an all-weather jet interceptor. Later, in 1957, there would come Sputnik, the Soviet space satellite, but long before then the argument that brainpower bred security had become commonplace.

That was not all. Education was, potentially, wealth. Putting money into education was the same as putting money into a low-risk, high-yield investment portfolio. In its purest form the argument went something like this:

. . . if our future wealth depends on education so that expenditure on education is properly looked on as investment likely to yield a high economic return, our growing wealth makes it easier to accept the cost of education without reference to that economic return.[1]

This was, to put it mildly, an argument attractive to government. It was attractive on several levels. Education in Canada, including university education, is the responsibility of the provinces. But for many years it has been accepted that the federal government has an interest in the fruits of education and in research, whether pure or applied. The federal government's attention could be attracted by the argument that education contributed to the nation's resources and thereby to the nation's defence. Besides, the federal government had a duty, newly discovered, to manage the Canadian economy according to the latest and best principles of economic science. It also helped that the federal cabinet and bureaucracy in the late 1940s and early 1950s contained several ex-professors. The Prime Minister, Louis St. Laurent, had taught law. The Minister of Trade and Commerce, C. D. Howe, had taught engineering. The Minister of External Affairs, Lester B. Pearson, had taught history. So had the Prime Minister's factotum, J. W. Pickersgill. Even the Governor General was a sometime and part-time member of the professoriate. Many of their counterparts in the universities – deans, presidents, and principals – had seen service in Ottawa. They knew how to ring the chimes and bang the gongs, and for the first time they had an attentive and appreciative audience.

Just at the appropriate moment, in 1951, a federal Royal Commission on National Development in the Arts, Letters and Sciences, chaired by Vincent Massey, bellied forth its own recommendations, arguing for direct federal aid to the universities on the grounds that the latter played "a national role." They were "recruiting

14

grounds for the national services," military and civil. They had made and were making a "great contribution ... to the defence of our country through the fundamental research work which they undertook during the war, and are continuing in the perilous times in which we live." The Commission went even further: "Scientific research is essential to material well-being and national security; the universities gave it birth, without them it would die."[2]

Help, tangible help, followed swiftly. In June 1951 the federal government announced direct grants to the nation's universities. There was no consultation with the provinces, but only one province, Quebec, took the drastic step of instructing its universities, after a year's grace period, to turn them down. What happened? In 1948-49 universities met 56 per cent of their costs either from fees or from endowment income. The provincial governments contributed less than a third. (The remainder was made up of federal aid to veterans of the Second World War, a temporary phenomenon.) Twenty years later, in 1968-69, the picture was very different. Now student fees plus endowment income contributed about a quarter of universities' income. Government supplied the rest.

By the beginning of the 1980s the picture had changed even more. Most Canadian universities now receive as much as 90 per cent of their funding directly from provincial governments and student fees contribute as little as 8 per cent. Endowments, once a major factor in university funding, are now far less important. The new universities that sprang up in the 1960s have endowment funds that are positively tiny compared to total university budgets. Older institutions, such as McGill University, have been forced to husband endowment funds, which now cover less and less of their budgets that skyrocketed during the heady days of ex-

15

pansion. Universities, today, are extensions of provincial ministries of higher or advanced education.

Provincial governments do not foot the bill alone. Federal contributions to universities' finance started off at 12 per cent of operating revenues in 1951 and ended up at 17 per cent in 1966-67. They rose from roughly $7 million to $99 million in the same period. These were sizable sums, and there is no doubt that the universities put them to good and immediate use. For one thing, nobody had to be fired as costs rose and student bodies failed to increase by very much in the early 1950s. For another, a moderate number of junior faculty could be recruited to replace the pre-1914 generation as it shuffled off into penury and retirement. But federal contributions were not all. Provincial grants to universities began to grow, too, helped in part by fiscal incentives from Ottawa. By 1961-62 student fees, that old standby of university finance, had shrunk to 23.5 per cent of revenues, while grants from provincial governments had risen to 28 per cent.

Provincial governments had begun to catch on. They were assisted by rapidly growing revenues, and they were encouraged to take action by the knowledge that in a very few years the number of young Canadians of university age – the "baby boom" of the forties and fifties – would be of college age. More Canadians than ever before were in high school. More were coming up through the elementary schools. It was safe to predict that more would be qualified for university entrance, and soon. It did not take much imagination to know that Canada's youth, and their voting parents, could and would look across the forty-ninth parallel at the great state mass education systems of the United States. By the late 1950s enrolments were going up at the rate of 12, 13, and 10 per cent per annum, and university expenditures were matching them. The less than 70,000 students of 1954 became the 141,000 students of 1962 and the 266,000 students of 1968.

Existing universities grew almost exponentially. Since by themselves they could hardly hope to accommodate the incoming mob, the old were supplemented by new plantations. There wasn't much time in which to make the necessary decisions, but for once the forecasters did not lie. There were plenty of student bodies to be housed and stimulated, and there would continue to be for the medium term. It was not the forecasters' fault if, in the middle of the greatest expansion of college classrooms ever seen in Canada, Canada's affluent young moderns started experimenting with another wonder of the twentieth century, the birth-control pill. In the mid-1960s the birth rate started to fall (particularly in Quebec), and the supply of potential students began to dry up. It would take time, much time, for the effects to reach the university. It would not, however, take quite as much time for the politicians to notice the effects and to draw appropriate conclusions.

Boom and Bust

The Canadian university system reached its apogee in the 1960s and early 1970s. It benefited from prosperity, from the availability of students, and from the decision by provincial governments to educate those students. "No person in this country who has the potential to make good in the university world ... should be denied that education," Ontario Premier Leslie Frost proclaimed in 1958. Most Canadian politicians agreed with him, or at least thought it imprudent to disagree.

Universities therefore became another form of government largesse to be laid before a grateful flock of voters. It was creative largesse. Universities sprouted in more and more improbable places: Lethbridge, St. Catharines, Chicoutimi, and Nelson. Where colleges had existed before, usually under religious auspices, there was a mass conversion to secularism – and grants. Baptists, Lutherans, Catholics all joined the stampede to the public trough. Few indeed were the religious who stayed outside the ambit of public funding and those few, usually fundamentalists or Calvinists or the purest and barest forms of religious professional training, passed almost unnoticed. Quebec, under the impetus of the so-called Quiet Revolution, evolved a complete Université du Québec with campuses spread from Rimouski to Hull. Quebec also created a compulsory junior college system (CEGEPs), to which students from inside the province were obliged to go before they could be admitted to the university proper.

Citizens in the towns where universities sprouted viewed them as a source of civic pride and local importance. They may have had second thoughts when, in the late 1960s, many Canadian campuses gave themselves over to the noisier forms of radical politics. But when, in the mid-1970s, the Canadian economy began to falter, numbers of Canadian towns and small cities discovered that with local industry shutting down the largest remaining employer in sight was the local college or university. Because these institutions were directly supported by provincial governments, it followed that pressure could be put on provincial politicians to keep the relevant college open. In this case colleges and universities were no different from airports, air bases, aircraft factories, or other recipients of government subsidies. Those examples chosen had all once been considered, in the 1940s and 1950s, to be the leading edge of society's quest for self-improvement and economic prosperity. In the 1970s and 1980s they had become job creation schemes, impossible to close because of the hardship their shutdown would cause.

The burden – the political burden at any rate – fell almost entirely on provincial governments because, in 1966, the federal government had bowed out of direct grants to Canadian universities. Instead of grants that then averaged $5 per capita there would now be transfer payments to the provinces according to an agreed formula – $15 per capita or 50 per cent of university operating costs – and the provinces would hand them on to the universities. In 1983, these transfer payments were about $4 billion. It was not quite the end of direct federal interest in universities; there continued to be funds for specialized research, grants to faculty, and a student aid program, but there would be no more money for ordinary operating expenses. In future the universities would have only one principal paymaster, the provinces.

"He who pays the piper calls the tune." So it had been before the 1960s; so it would be again. During the 1960s governments had wanted universities to expand, and they had been joined in that wish by university administrations and faculties. There were jobs for everybody. There were contracts for architects to build concrete and glass boxes on once-pleasant residential streets or in muddy cow pastures. There were jobs for faculty to fill the boxes, and as there were not enough Canadian faculty to go around, thanks to the starvation policies of the late 1940s and early 1950s, new professors were imported, most often from the United States. The shortages of staff also filtered into the consciousness of governments, and the result was a dramatic rise in faculty salaries and conditions of employment.

This was natural enough, since university teachers were a scarce commodity and the provinces were bidding in a seller's market.

The sheer size of the increase deserves some notice. In a generation, from 1960 to 1983, the numbers of Canadian university faculty rose from 7,760 to 33,000. There were also almost 20,000 teachers in community colleges. These professors and teachers were instructing a body of students that was still growing: more than 350,000 in the early 1980s. This was only natural, since the effects of the birth-control pill had still not worked their way into post-secondary education. They had, however, done so in the secondary schools, and the indirect results in the university were very great. Teaching jobs in the secondary school systems grew very scarce. This had a direct impact at the universities, where enrolments dropped in teacher-training courses. There was thus no longer any need for students to take some of the humanities or social science subjects in the university for vocational purposes. With the collapse of secondary school recruitment, then, universities lost a significant and traditionally central part of their clientele. This was a fact with some political significance, for the province was no longer under much pressure to maintain the teacher-training system when there was an oversupply of teachers roaming around – and teachers' colleges closed or consolidated.

Demographic pressures had created a large and somewhat decentralized university system. This had occurred because politicians sensed that university education, with its consequent entrée to high status and high salary occupations, was what the people wanted. The people got what they wanted, and in fairly short order. The initial cost was high, but it could be justified in terms of decades or even generations of use. Nobody, or practically nobody, expected the population trends to reverse themselves, nor was such a reversal expected just at the point when the great thirty-year post-war economic boom crunched to a halt.

Hard Times on the Campus

The late 1970s and early 1980s have not been the best of times to be on a Canadian university campus. Trapped inside a patron-client relationship with government that they themselves had dreamt about and helped to create, Canadian universities were ill-prepared and ill-adapted to meet the funding crunch that provincial governments imposed on them.

True, the descent from the heights was gradual and not entirely painful. University professors earned a great deal of money, comparatively speaking, in the early 1970s. So, for that matter, did other professionals, such as doctors and lawyers, who earned much more than professors. The hard times of the war and post-war periods were over, and professors had recovered almost to the heights of the balmy 1920s. There were only two differences: first, there were many more professors, and second, universities were now far more dependent on the provinces for their sustenance.

It was natural that universities met the problem of diminishing government grants by recourse to invisible funding. Repairs were not made as quickly, or were made not at all (older universities with older buildings suffered most from this). Equipment was not replaced. Scholarly journals were closed down. Professors were told not to mount new courses that might oblige the university library to buy new books, or multiple copies of books. Young faculty members were put onto "revolving door" contracts, known in the trade as contractually limited appointments, or CLTAs. Thanks to Canada's high rate of inflation, faculty salaries continued to increase in the late 1970s – a full professor in Ontario was paid in the $50,000 range – but in real, constant dollar terms they were shrinking.

The shrinkage of university resources in real terms did not, however, coincide with a collapse in enrolment. Quite the contrary. Canada's youth, for whatever reason, continued to go to university or to other forms of post-secondary education. Class sizes, therefore, showed a tendency to grow larger although certain programs, such as graduate studies in the arts and sciences, began to shrink. Professional faculties boomed, a phenomenon that put pressure on resources allocated to "arts" or even "science" subjects.

In a country as diverse as Canada it cannot be expected that university funding or expenditures followed the same pattern everywhere. Ontario, which had led the ascent to the ivory tower, now led the descent. By the early 1980s, although it was by no means the poorest province, Ontario was tenth in per capita expenditures on universities. It was well known that Ontario faculty salaries were lagging, and lagging to such a degree that it was assumed to be impossible to pay anyone fortunate enough to teach in western Canada a matching salary in Ontario. (As a rule of thumb, one can assume a 10 to 20 per cent salary gap.) Quebec, on the other hand, enjoyed a Parti Québécois government, which assumed that it represented, among others, the French-speaking professoriate and, as a consequence, Quebec faculty salaries grew until the Quebec government finally called a halt and imposed a salary reduction. In British Columbia the government in 1983 introduced an ambitious program that would, among other things, alter the conditions of employment at that province's universities. It is still too soon to know whether B.C.'s restraint package will have any special impact on the universities, although the province intends to cut grants to the universities by 5 per cent in 1984. That will mean salary cuts.

These are the surface consequences of under-funding, and they are serious enough. Canada's universities, having ceased to grow, do not know how to shrink. Even if, in some unlikely scenario, the universities were prepared to take surgical action, it is doubtful that governments would let them do what they desired: the lines of subsidy that lead from the campus to provincial treasuries are also lines of control.

The variations in funding schemes that exist across the country are complicated, and it is not worth our while to explore them here. As a general and obvious rule, it is accepted that larger universities get more money. Government funding to an institution in most provinces is still substantially based on the number of students the place can cram in, although sometimes governments have placed restrictions on the numbers and types of students a university can accommodate. But the governments, fighting inflation with cutbacks in funding, have usually increased their university grants by much less than enough to keep up with the rise in the cost-of-living index. Nonetheless, the universities were not slow to understand that they had better get out and hustle up warm, breathing, basic income units. Recruiters began to scour the countryside in search of a hinterland. Faculty members were assigned to high school duty so as to present a "human face" to their potential recruits. Advertisements in newspapers were natural recruiting devices, and so were commercials on TV and radio. Admission standards, admittedly uncertain, were lowered to provide every young citizen who could write his or her own name and command an inflated 60 per cent average out of high school the opportunity to sup with Plato and dine with Descartes. Or at least with their worthy substitutes from St. John's to Victoria.

An enrolment-based funding policy, therefore, helped to generate policies and politics all its own. Since it coincided, unhappily, with the end of standardized province-wide high school testing it meant that there was a very real uncertainty in the universities as to who would be knocking next at the professorial door. One or two universities tried to protect themselves by failing high proportions of their first-year students (much as engineering faculties had been doing for years), who thereby became basic income units in a very real sense. Others eventually imposed language-proficiency testing. What was being tested, in fact, was illiteracy, though nobody was impolite enough to use the term officially. These two methods of containing, though not curing, the problem of inappropriate admissions caused surprisingly little comment. The cloak of university autonomy could be drawn round the unpleasant spectacle and since what was going on was internal to the university it could hardly embarrass interests outside the university.

But what of cases where a university imposed admission standards of its own, standards that might possibly indicate that the quality of education received by its high school recruits was, shall we say, somewhat deficient? Those, alas, are the proverbial horses of a different colour. When the University of Toronto announced in 1982 that it would, after a judicious lapse of time, refuse to count certain rubbishy and irrelevant high school subjects as qualifications for admission, it was not slow to learn whose ox was being gored. The teachers' federations naturally objected. Their members, after all, taught courses in the relevant discipline. What did it matter that one of the subjects was an amalgam of home economics and pseudo-sociology travelling under the title "The Canadian Family"? Surely "family" students were entitled to be considered to the same degree and proportion as those taking, say, calculus or geography or Latin? Not only teachers objected. So did school boards and their administrators. Officials of the university were made aware, in no uncertain terms, of the dudgeon of the local educators and reminded that there was a direct connection between the prosperity and even existence of their university and the benevolent feelings that high school teachers might hold toward it.

Such examples could be multiplied. It may be pointless now to apportion blame for a situation when universities become recruitment road shows, or when prosperity and even survival depend on the warm and feely image a university projects. The universities invited it when they agreed to a form of funding that embodied a numbers game. They accepted an annual lottery, and then they attempted to fiddle with the rules. The provincial politicians, viewing university as a government-funded consumer benefit, naturally tried to extend a college education to the largest possible number and, when their funds contracted, to do it at the least possible expense to the provincial taxpayer. Up to a point, at least, the universities and their provincial masters could point to the proud democratic motto of equal accessibility.

It is, however, hard to believe that the present situation could possibly have been what Leslie Frost was talking about in 1958 when he proclaimed the government's duty to see that any qualified student capable of benefiting from a university education got one. From the perspective of the fifties, Frost probably meant a university system that would continue to admit a small minority of the available students. He would not have expected perfection – he was too much of a realist for that – but he would have assumed that reasonable standards would be imposed to keep the illiterates out.

It is not surprising that the public is beginning to realize that Canadian children are being ill-educated. The statement by the province of Alberta in 1983 that it was reimposing province-wide high school leaving exams, the holding of the first examinations in January 1984, and the announcement by the Ottawa Board of Education that it was considering a city-wide examination system were straws in the wind. It may be anticipated that other jurisdictions will follow.

This development should not be unwelcome to the university. Nevertheless, it should not be forgotten that the reappearance after decades of neglect of a uniform admissions qualification is far from a complete solution to the universities' dilemma. It leaves intact the funding system that created the dilemma in the first place, and it leaves unanswered the question of what, exactly, is to be done with all those professors made redundant by the disappearance of large numbers of unqualified students.

The solution to this question can only be political, but because there are so many highly dangerous factors involved it is not to be supposed that the politicians will wish to grasp at it. They have, by now, learned that universities are expensive propositions. Their answer, by and large, has been to cut down on funding without offering much guidance to the universities on how they should trim and pare. Universities, therefore, have cut everywhere, at the cost of damaging faculty morale, their own physical plant, the quality of education they offer, and their books and equipment. The same swingeing process has occurred at universities major and minor, for in the age of equality all are equal, and therefore all are equally subject to cuts. It is well known that the voters of Lethbridge or Rimouski would resent and would punish at the polls a policy that singled out their small university for special reductions; and the same process applies in Brandon, Montreal, Halifax, Peterborough, Sherbrooke, and elsewhere in Canada.

The perspective that political control over the universities offers is therefore utterly dismal. The university system of Canada, and of each single province, has been paralysed at the point of its maximum growth. It is not, as a deliberate matter of government policy, to be permitted to shrink very much. It will be allowed to starve a bit, and while starving, to feed on gruel produced by the provincial treasuries. The effect will be to keep the dependent universities weak and starving, but not so transparently so as to cause distress to the average elector. And there will probably be no funerals, because policy forbids it. It may be that a limb of one part of the system will be lopped off and grafted on another part, and it may even be that expenditure will be reduced thereby. Such a policy will at best be mere tinkering, and it will ignore the possibility that diminishing resources could be differently allocated for a different effect.

What will exist in this skeletal framework? An aging faculty, trapped by its own optimism, its own commitment, and its own short-sightedness. (There will, however, be lots of them.) Students receiving an increasingly second-class education, which by its nature cannot fit them to meet international standards of competition. (There may even be lots of students, too.) Universities, no single one of which will be strong enough in terms of faculty, research, or resources to offer a proper education, far less to serve as a "national resource" of the kind the Massey Royal Commission on the Arts, Letters and Sciences projected in the early 1950s. (But there will be plenty of universities.)

What will not be there? Exceptional scholars and

scientists. The former will leave if they can and, if they cannot, will retreat to an inner-directed seclusion. The scientists, more mobile, will presumably leave, or will seek employment directly with government or industry. Talented undergraduates with money will flee the country for opportunity and education abroad. They are already en route to Yale, Harvard, and Princeton.

Very simply, the universities are in a financial mess, and the problems are simply horrendous. One of the first things that must be done is to find some way of changing the present basis of funding. No longer can it be tied to enrolments in any way, for the experience with that kind of system has been disastrous. Undoubtedly, some contraction in the large systems will be necessary – if not of universities then of programs. There is no reason for each and every university to have a graduate program in every discipline nor for a province like Ontario to have law schools in Ottawa, Toronto (2), London, Kingston, and Windsor – particularly when there are more lawyers now than society can tolerate. The money that might be saved in this way could go to the universities to re-build their physical plants, restock their laboratories, and possibly even bring real faculty salaries to the level they were at five or ten years ago.

There must be an end to the open accessibility that has ruined the universities. Incompetent students, students who should never have gone to university, have nearly destroyed the system. Standards once again must be applied, and if this means entrance exams or a return to provincial high school leaving exams, so be it. Anything is better than the present situation. This is an elitist solution, we recognize, but at the same time, the provinces have to create a vast scheme of scholarships (not bursaries or loans) so that all students of talent, rich or poor, have a chance to get all the education they can handle. Anything less will be a scandal.

And the students who come to the university will have to pay higher fees. Education in Canada, even in its present state, is a bargain particularly when compared to tuition costs in the United States. Students should pay a higher percentage of the costs of their education. This is important because fees, now such a small part in university budgets, are funds that are not directly controlled by the provincial governments. Discretionary funds from increased tuition might let some universities make themselves marginally different from others, might let them enhance their quality departments, and might give the institutions some flexibility that is sadly lacking now.

These changes are not earthshaking, but they are important. The certainty is that some major changes in the funding sector are necessary. And it is absolutely certain that the universities cannot survive as long as every student, regardless of his scholastic abilities, has the right to attend.

Notes

[1] The Bladen Report, quoted in University Affairs (November, 1965), p. 1.

[2] The Report of the Royal Commission on National Development in the Arts, Letters and Sciences (Ottawa, 1951)

CHAPTER III

Internal Democracy and the Road to Hell

Canadian universities strive to be models of democracy. The old elitist structures of an earlier era have mostly been swept away in a drive that was intended to reform, reorganize, and regenerate higher education in Canada. The university senate, the highest academic body in the institution and responsible for deciding virtually all academic and pedagogical matters, was reformed over a decade ago with heavy representation added from administrators and students as well as teaching staff. Relations between faculty and boards of governors are now dominated by trade unionism and collective bargaining. These developments may be beneficial to the cause of Canadian democracy; nonetheless, they are paving the road to hell in higher education. Unless the process is somehow reversed the nature of Canadian universities will be fundamentally altered – for the worse – and the quality of higher education will be drastically altered.

Labour Relations: Institutionalized Warfare

Labour law and collective bargaining practices have been developing in Canada at the federal and provincial level since 1872 when the government of Prime Minister John A. Macdonald passed the Trades Union

Act. That bill allowed trade unions to exist legally for the first time, giving workers the right to organize collectively for defence against their employers and the advancement of their economic interests. Since 1872 workers have had their rights progressively expanded, governments and employers have come to accept unions (however reluctantly), and labour law and collective bargaining have become highly complex and institutionalized. The aim of government – and most unions – is to institutionalize the obvious conflict of interest between employers and workers. Employers, as rational economic men, want to keep as much of their profits as possible. Their workers, also rational economic men, want to maximize their earnings. The result was, and is, conflict, sometimes violent and bloody, that might well have toppled the capitalist system if not channelled and institutionalized by labour law.

Our collective bargaining system was designed to accommodate the needs of employers and workers in industry; it sets the rules for an institutionalized warfare, draws the boundaries of the conflict, and referees the struggle. And struggle it must be, because it is based on the assumption that although the interests of employers and workers overlap, bosses and their workers will invariably clash. This has led to the development of large and complex collective agreements that govern all aspects of the relationship between these parties over the life of the agreement. Little is left to chance, informality, or custom. In these days of high-priced lawyers, industrial relations experts, and labour relations boards with quasi-judicial powers, a handshake is no longer enough. This is the world that most Canadian university professors have entered with little thought about the horrendous implications that faculty trade unionism will have for higher education.

Good-bye Mr. Chips

Mr. Chips no longer exists in the modern Canadian university. Tweed jackets with leather elbow patches abound, as do pipes and cardigans, but the stooped, bespectacled, sherry-sipping professor, deferential to a fault and quaking with fear at a harsh word from the dean, is gone. Across the country the war babies now dominate the faculty and they have changed the demographic composition of the profession and its ethnic and socio-economic background. The changes came slowly at first but were well on their way by the mid-1960s when the Canadian Association of University Teachers and the Association of Universities and Colleges of Canada commissioned a study of university governance by Sir James Duff, formerly vice-chancellor of the University of Durham in England, and Robert O. Berdahl, a professor at San Francisco State College. From one end of the country to another, it was increasingly clear that there was something vitally wrong with the way universities were being governed (at least in the minds of students and a growing number of professors) and that some hard, objective look was necessary to find the cause of the problems and recommend solutions. This came before the tidal wave of student revolt swept across Canada, but there was already the example of student revolt in the United States and Europe. It was also clear that professors were beginning to chafe at their lack of authority in academic matters, their inability to influence important budgeting and funding decisions, and their powerlessness at the hands of boards of governors that often appeared to have little understanding of, or sympathy for, what the faculty saw as the true objectives of high education.

The new generation of professors had grown up in the post-war world of super consumption, political liberality, the growth of social welfare institutions, and the spread of multiculturalism. They saw the rapid rise of other professions, such as medicine and law, to positions of unchallenged wealth, power, and authority in Canadian society – usually because of the self-regulation and self-government bestowed on them by provincial governments – and they believed they were powerless peons in comparison. Faculty associations thus began to demand a greater share in the power to make the vital academic, budgetary, and administrative decisions that determined the course of higher education. They, too, were professionals, like doctors and lawyers, but they did not receive the respect, esteem, and high earning power that seemed to go with professionalism. Duff and Berdahl were charged with finding a way to satisfy faculty demands.

The two commissioners toured the country in the first half of 1965 interviewing professors, administrators, and students and studying the structure of university government in large and small institutions. They found "unnecessarily high degrees of tension within the larger institutions" and a "fairly widespread desire on the part of the smaller universities to expand and inherit the problems of their larger sisters."[1] The present system, they concluded, needed reform and they recommended changes at the highest and most important levels of university government, from the boards of governors down.

Duff and Berdahl found a haphazard system of lay-dominated boards of governors, senates chosen in a variety of ways, and administrative structures built around the university president. The system had first developed in the 1830s out of the civic universities of England, such as the University of London. Those institutions did not have the financial independence of the separate colleges that made up Oxford and Cambridge and, therefore, lay-dominated boards were needed to raise funds and direct spending. This, quite naturally, limited the independence of professors who, at Oxford and Cambridge, dominated university government to such a degree that they were, for all intents and purposes, totally independent and totally self-governing in their institutions.

Duff and Berdahl recognized that the Oxford and Cambridge model could not be applied to Canada – they did not think it worked all that well in any case – and they accepted the need for boards of governors that would represent and protect the public interest in universities, and for senates, composed of teaching staff and some administrators, to make academic decisions. Duff and Berdahl believed that the composition of the boards and senates they examined was not well defined, however. There was too much overlap in authority between these two bodies and the exact role of each was not clearly laid out. Boards had tended to dominate universities and administrators had tended to dominate senates, leaving disgruntled teaching staff to complain that they were allowed little say in running their universities.

Duff and Berdahl recommended that boards, senates, and the administration be reorganized. Boards, they suggested, should have direct faculty representation chosen from the senate and indirect student representation with students choosing a non-student "Rector" to represent them. They realized that some board members would object to faculty representation on the grounds that the board was an employer and faculty were employees, but Duff and Berdahl explicitly rejected this: "The normal employer-employee relationship . . . cannot apply in a university, where the profit motive does not and ought not to exist and where productivity simply is not measurable."[2] There was, therefore, no reason why faculty should be excluded from boards and every reason to have them on – faculty members knew the university "from the inside" and could add considerable insight to board deliberations, Duff and Berdahl suggested.

Duff and Berdahl wanted the board to remain the ultimate *de jure* authority for the university and to be responsible for the business side of university affairs. They believed the board had to work closely with the senate on most matters and should not have power to overrule the senate on educational questions. The senate, therefore, would be responsible primarily for academic affairs and, as such, should have a majority of members elected by the academic staff with some representation from the administration. The president and his staff were to form the main bridge between the board and the senate, which had to work together, in harness, to direct the university. The Duff-Berdahl recommendations were labeled "shared authority," became the model, in the mid to late 1960s, for university government throughout Canada, and were written into provincial university charters and acts of incorporation. One major exception to the Duff-Berdahl recommendations that became common practice was the granting of full student representation on university senates. Duff and Berdahl discussed this in their report, noted that it was being experimented with at some institutions in Canada and the United States, but stopped short of recommending it.

Their recommendations were based on the idea that the university was a community of scholars who shared basic interests. Duff and Berdahl therefore discouraged the practice of appointing deans and department heads with long periods of tenure and suggested, instead, regular rotation on a relatively short-term basis for both. This would ensure that academics not only taught but also ran departments and faculties and then returned to the teaching ranks when their job was done. Duff and Berdahl saw no necessary adversarial relationship between administrators and professors nor between boards and professors. But they were wrong; the system they had proposed began to break down almost as soon as it became widespread at Canadian universities.

Dollar Scarcity, Scholar Militancy

As with so many things in life, it began over money. In the days of the Great Academic Barbecue – roughly 1962 to 1972 – university enrolment jumped every year as the baby boom flooded on to the campuses. As student enrolment swelled, as more classrooms and lecture halls were added, as greater sums of government dollars were force-fed into higher education, professorial salaries jumped by leaps and bounds and the demands for new staff created a seller's market. Academic salaries had tumbled in real terms during the 1930s and 1940s and, although they had improved somewhat since then, they remained very low until the mid-1960s when they began to grow exponentially. Not only did salary levels grow, but many of the new generation of professors (willing to switch jobs, institutions, and cities almost yearly) were able to leapfrog into ever higher salary ranks without having to prove themselves either as scholars or teachers. The threat of departure was often enough to send a department head scurrying to the dean for a salary increase for the latest "promising young scholar" who had joined the department from some prominent graduate school clutching a sheaf of glowing recommendations from professors of alleged national and international repute. There was no end to the upward spiral. The Horn of Plenty gave and gave.

36

The annual Learned Societies meetings became like the winter baseball flesh markets; recruiting, not the presentation of scholarly papers, was the most important activity.

And then it stopped short at the beginning of the 1970s. The baby boom went bust. Enrolments at most universities flattened out and even began to decline for several years. Universities began to impose hiring freezes as governments began talking about restraint. Suddenly there were many more graduate students than available jobs. Suddenly there was no mobility. Suddenly the "promising young scholars" had to stand and deliver. Many could not. The vast majority were stuck where they had landed and feared an uncertain future as administrations and boards, too quick to do the governments' work, began to threaten wholesale dismissals of staff, even those with tenure, as part of the cutback strategy for the new scarcity of the 1970s.

One of the great flaws in the Duff-Berdahl structure was now revealed: there was little or no provision for dealing with the breakdown in shared authority that came with the budget crunches. Duff and Berdahl had believed that boards were necessary to safeguard the public interest and direct the financial life of the universities. Perhaps they are. But boards, then and now, are dominated by businessmen and lawyers who, whatever their understanding of the uniqueness of the university, naturally act like businessmen and lawyers. That is not necessarily a bad thing, especially when times are good, but it can be a very bad thing when times get bad, quickly. What began to happen across Canada in the early 1970s was that boards of governors began to act like company boards of directors with little sympathy for, or understanding of, faculty concerns. And university administrators, even those with strong faculty backgrounds themselves, began to act like personnel managers. Panic buttons were hit as boards and administrators declared that their sacred trust to protect the taxpayers' interests would not be violated. It did not occur to most of these people that there were better ways of protecting those interests than threatening wholesale dismissals of tenured staff without even bothering to prove that a real budget crisis existed (in most cases it did not, at least not in the early 1970s). Faculty across Canada were almost forced to assume a defensive posture and, in their growing fear, they demanded a better way.

Out of this grew the thrust toward collective bargaining. The sudden need for job security, combined with the realization that salary dollars were going to become much harder to get, prompted many of the younger members of university faculties across the country to forsake the shared-authority ideals of Duff and Berdahl and quickly to adopt the "we-they" thinking that boards were also accepting. It was a vicious circle, and although the structures of the Duff-Berdahl recommendations remained intact – and are still at most Canadian universities – the spirit of those ideals quickly dissipated.

The Slippery Slope to Faculty Unionism

In the beginning, there was collective begging, not collective bargaining. Although Duff and Berdahl had elaborated a model for shared authority in Canadian universities, they were almost silent on the matter of how salaries and economic benefits were to be determined. They believed boards should continue to hold supreme power in such matters, but they acknowledged that "a necessary function" of faculty associations was to request "consideration of salary scales or conditions of [employment],"[3] leaving the impression that the academic staff, like old-time factory hands, were to approach the board, cap in hand, when the time came to set salaries. Perhaps Duff and Berdahl believed that a smoothly functioning system of shared authority would not create a "we-they" relationship, that a university in which academic staff, administrators, and board worked together in harmony would not be the scene for disputes over salary and other mundane matters. If so, they were wrong. The standard procedure for salary determination in the 1960s was, in fact, cap in hand, but that did not seem to matter as long as the gravy train was running smoothly. The salary crisis that developed at the University of Alberta in early 1970 was the first major indication, however, that the amicability that had marked board-faculty association discussions over salary, and which the Duff-Berdahl cap-in-hand system depended on, was rapidly disappearing.

The University of Alberta in the late 1960s was a model of Duff-Berdahl relationships. Each year the faculty, acting through the Association of Academic Staff of the University of Alberta (AASUA), presented a salary brief to the board, the board and the AASUA met to discuss salaries, and, after several months, the board would set the new salary scales after considerable consultation with AASUA. In late 1969, however, with a budget crisis apparently looming, the board and the AASUA ran into heavy going, and after eight to nine months the board unilaterally promulgated the new salary scales. The velvet glove turned out to have an iron fist in it after all.

The AASUA met in the spring of 1970 to decide its next course of action. After studying several options, it chose to seek voluntary recognition from the board of governors to bargain collectively and to resort to a system of final-offer selection in case of a future impasse with the board over salaries. In this system an independent arbitrator, chosen by both parties, then selects the final position of one of the two sides as the final arbitration award. The idea behind final-offer selection is that the arbitrator will not simply split the difference between the parties but will choose the most reasonable solution. Both parties, therefore, will be kept honest. After gaining the support of the faculty and the senate (it is called the General Faculties Council in Alberta) the AASUA convinced the board to go along with this and, in September 1971, the University of Alberta became the first major campus in English Canada to utilize a system of collective bargaining in determining salaries. It was a new departure even though it did not involve unionization and the staff explicitly rejected the right to strike.

By choice or by necessity (faculty unions are illegal in British Columbia and Alberta), some university faculty associations followed the voluntary recognition procedures of the University of Alberta, but most did not. They were not content with the questionable legal protection that voluntary recognition brought – a board that voluntarily recognized a faculty association could just as voluntarily unrecognize it – nor with the generally restricted list of subjects for bargaining in such a system. It was not enough to bargain over salaries and fringe benefits, reasoned many young faculty association leaders; they wanted to nail the board down to legally enforceable contracts that covered all aspects of the working relationship between the board and the academic staff. And thus the rush to unionization began. By the spring of 1976 it was well on its way. At that point faculty unions had been certified at the four campuses of the Université du Québec, St. Mary's University in Halifax, Notre Dame University in Nelson, British Columbia (which has since been closed by the

B.C. government), the University of Manitoba, the Université de Laval, the Université de Sherbrooke, the Université de Montréal, the University of Ottawa, Carleton University, York University, Bishop's University, and Algoma University College, while certification was pending at three other campuses. Almost one-third of 25,000 faculty members in Canada had become members of certified bargaining agents. Today, there is a solid majority.

At individual universities, faculty members wrestled with the implications of unionization. Their leaders sincerely believed that unionism would bring equality with administrators and boards, fair grievance procedures, and higher pay. They worried about the possibility of unionization affecting the strictly academic side of the university and various compromises were attempted at different campuses to make sure that bargaining was restricted to salary and fringe benefits, working conditions, and determining the procedures for deciding who was to be hired, promoted, allowed to go on leave, and dismissed. Those compromises have rarely worked; it is almost impossible to bargain about how to set up procedures without also affecting the academic decisions themselves that are arrived at under those procedures.

The Canadian Association of University Teachers gave precious little thought or leadership in weighing the possible impact of unionization on academic life, the purposes of a university, or the quality of higher education. Although the Bulletin of the Canadian Association of University Teachers published a dozen or more articles on collective bargaining and/or unionization (which are not necessarily the same thing) between the spring of 1968 and the spring of 1976, most were concerned with the "how" of the matter, not the possible ramifications of it. From the very start, the CAUT accepted collective bargaining and unionization as methods it believed could help attain its objectives of greater power and protection for faculty. There was, however, no open and sustained discussion in the pages of the CAUT *Bulletin* or at the annual CAUT meetings about the merits of unionization when viewed from an educational point of view. The talk was strictly economic. And even from an economic perspective few faculty associations heeded the suggestions of B. L. Adell and D. D. Carter[4] that boards were not, in any case, financially independent and that faculty should consider bargaining directly with provincial governments.

Faculty went after the boards because the boards were present on the campus and visible and because many boards acted like robber barons toward their faculty. But boards were then and are now the wrong target. Provincial governments give fixed annual grants to the boards. The faculty then try to lever as much as possible out of the boards using their newly discovered bargaining power. Every dollar that then goes to faculty salaries and fringe benefits from this fixed sum is a dollar that does not go to libraries, computer operations, and so on. The boards have virtually no independent source of operating funds and the universities are stuck (along with the staff) in a vicious circle. Too large a salary settlement can mean (and has meant) layoffs, dismissals, and cutbacks in important areas of institutional spending. Boards and faculty unions go round and round, like hamsters on a treadmill, while provincial ministers of higher education, the real robber barons, remain aloof and untouched.

Playing in the Big, Tough World

Faculty unions do not, of course, bargain only about salaries – they must by law bargain about almost everything. It no longer matters whether Duff and Berdahl were correct in asserting that a university was not a factory. It most certainly is a factory as far as a labour relations board is concerned. There is only one set of labour laws in each province, and it is applied to university professors just as it is applied to carpenters or sanitation workers. Thus, board-faculty contracts must fulfil the strict requirements of labour law and the rules of labour relations boards before they can become legally binding. Such contracts now run well over one hundred pages at most universities with faculty unions, and they define every aspect of the working relationship between the board and the faculty. Many faculty members welcome this and believe they finally have the protection they have always needed. This is certainly the view of the CAUT, which takes the position that the contractual definition of board-faculty relations has increased faculty influence and enhanced fairness in procedures, forced the board to come clean in bargaining for salaries, and ensured that dismissals for financial reasons are not carried out in an arbitrary way. There is some merit to these arguments. But the price for the achievement of this security has been and will be heavy; in the long run it may not be worth the cost.

Labour law and labour relations boards developed to regulate the naturally adversarial relationship between factory owners and their workers. Productivity is as measurable in the factory as is profitability, and this allows the system to work well enough in protecting the rights of workers, distributing an equitable share of the profits, and ensuring management's rights, which are based on the sacrosanct principle that those who own property are entitled, within the law, to control it and dispose of it as they please. It works well enough, but it does not work well. In the last decade more and more owners, workers, and labour relations experts have been studying other systems, such as the co-determination which is the practice in some European countries (a sort of Duff-Berdahl shared authority combined with trade unionism), to see if they can be applied here. But given the nature of the North American bargaining system – totally adversarial – there is too little trust to allow for such reforms. So far co-determination remains a dream.

At the very time that people in industry are examining co-determination, Canadian universities are leaving co-determination behind. And leaving it they are, because although senates continue in most institutions to carry the bulk of the decision-making load in academic matters, the collective agreement, based on a factory model, now governs everything else at a university. It lays out the procedures by which faculty are appointed, promoted, granted tenure, granted salary increases for meritorious performance, and dismissed for cause or for financial reasons. It gives faculty members the right to launch lengthy and costly grievances over almost everything including teaching assignment duties, faculty workload, the granting or denial of sabbaticals, and other matters. All this has a direct impact on the quality of the teaching staff and it can also have an impact on programs.

The union collective agreement may offer faculty protection in some areas, but it freezes faculty-board relations into a permanently adversarial relationship. Whatever chance shared authority might have had is disappearing. Boards that were already treating their professors in arbitrary ways have had their prejudices confirmed (even if their power has been reduced); those that were more enlightened have been stung into adversarial postures by certification. And many faculty have now started to accept the factory model as a normal working relationship and govern themselves accordingly. When the whistle blows at five, all tools are downed. This approach to higher education is already creeping onto university campuses.

Unionism may have been a boon for elementary and secondary school teacher salaries but it did nothing to improve the quality of teaching. The quality of the students that the schools are turning out, when measured by any of a number of tests, has declined markedly (see Chapter IV). Teachers tend to blame this on factors outside their control, but the attitudes, and the changes in those attitudes, brought about by unionization have had something to do with it. Teachers are no longer awarded merit increases in salary based on individual performance because their unions judge such increases unfair. Teachers now rarely perform extra duties for their students that are not specified in their union contract because their unions will not allow this; if they do they can be reprimanded. Secondary school teachers have been reprimanded by their unions for daring to speak out against certain of their union's practices. Teachers' unions are so determined to protect their members that other important considerations have fallen by the wayside. When an Eckville, Alberta, high school teacher was discovered to have taught – for thirteen years – that a world Jewish conspiracy controlled the history books and that Nazis never murdered Jews, the Alberta Teachers Association (ATA) helped him appeal his dismissal and a high ATA official told a television reporter that the teacher had a right to his own opinions in the classroom. It was many months before the ATA took any action at all to decertify this teacher. Can such things be far away at Canadian universities? University professors are no more intelligent, just, or tolerant than secondary school teachers and if teacher unionism provides an example of what the future holds on Canadian campuses, higher education in Canada is in for new and dangerous times.

Creeping Mediocrity

There are disturbing signs that the process has already started. Collective agreements at the University of Saskatchewan, York University, Laurentian University, and other institutions contain provisions about the granting of tenure, the distribution of merit pay, and dismissal for budgetary reasons that may be the thin edge of the wedge in discouraging excellence among university professors. Nothing is more important in the building of a qualified staff at a university than the decisions to grant tenure, to reward meritorious performance, and to provide job security for the best teachers and scholars. At the University of Saskatchewan, however, the collective agreement stipulates that when a faculty member is denied tenure, he not only has a right to appeal this decision to an appeals panel composed of his peers (an acceptable matter of fundamental justice), he also has the right to launch a grievance under the collective agreement. This gives an outside arbitrator the power to order the university to reconsider the matter and, in certain cases, to short-circuit the university's tenure-granting procedures and order tenure to be awarded. This is tenure by order, decided upon by a non-academic, on grounds that may have little or nothing to do with the competence of the candidate.

At York University, the collective agreement has effectively eliminated the awarding of merit pay. This is an additional salary award given for meritorious performance in teaching, service, or scholarship that enables the exceptional professor to earn more than those whose performance is average or worse. A merit system guarantees that a rough communism is not imposed on all academic staff and that those who deserve extra reward for their efforts get that extra reward. It is a system that holds out excellence as an ideal. Take away the merit reward, and the system then tells professors that they should be nothing more than teaching drones, expected only to put in X hours in front of a classroom. That is exactly what has happened throughout most universities in France – heavily unionized – where merit pay no longer exists and where scholarship is not encouraged because it is seen as detracting from the essential job of teaching. Those who are doing research and publishing spend just as much time teaching as those who are not, but the ideal demanded of university professors in Canada, at least up to now, has been to combine teaching, scholarship, and service to the university in roughly equal proportions. A university teacher is ideally a person who can and will contribute in all three areas. Scholarship and good teaching are directly related. Should scholarship be downplayed (not rewarding it is one excellent way of doing this), universities will become glorified high schools.

At Laurentian University the collective agreement stipulates that in case of a budget crunch, staff are to be laid off according to a formula heavily dependent on seniority. Other institutions have similar layoff procedures: at the University of Regina a complex formula is to be used to decide how much each department or faculty must cut from its budget and then faculty members are to be laid off strictly in conformity with seniority. At York University a strict order for layoffs is set out by the collective agreement, with non-tenured staff to be laid off first, followed by tenured staff. In both cases priority within each category is determined by seniority.

47

Seniority as a criterion for determining the order of layoffs is not in use in all university collective agreements, but it may well become so in time as potential financial crunches lead to actual firings. It is one of the best examples of how inappropriate the factory model is to universities. Seniority – the last hired will be the first fired – was adopted as standard practice in the North American industrial relations system many years ago as the fairest way of protecting the jobs and pension rights of senior employees who have given a larger proportion of their work lives to the company than those who were more junior to them. At the same time unions viewed it as the fairest way of protecting workers against arbitrary dismissal by the employer for suspicious reasons (such as trade union activity). Seniority works relatively well in a factory, especially those which are highly regulated and in which many workers perform similar tasks with little variance in skill or ability. A fifty-year-old welder who has given a company twenty years performs the same job, and probably with the same productivity, as the twenty-five-year-old welder standing next to him who has been employed only six months.

This is not, however, how a university is supposed to function. Professors are supposed to teach, do research, and perform services to the university on an individual basis and according to their ability. Some are better teachers than others, some do more and better research and scholarship than others; some are more valuable to the institution – to the students, to the university, to society at large – than others. When it comes to determining who is to be laid off in times of financial crisis these values must be the prime motivation in a university setting, not seniority. If people have to be laid off, and this is increasingly likely, then those who are not so good, those who are not so valuable to the university, those whose departure will be less damaging to the integrity of the institution and to the function of imparting knowledge should be the first to be laid off, not the youngest. Ability and age are not necessarily commensurate. Canadian universities should not be deciding who to keep and who to lay off by counting rings on a tree trunk. Seniority does violence to the very notion of a university.

Who should decide which faculty members are to be fired, if seniority is not to be used, and how should the decision be made? There is only one fair way. Each faculty in a university should be told how much it must cut from its budget by a university-wide committee composed of faculty members and representatives of faculty associations. The cuts within each faculty should be made by similar committees chosen on the same basis. Where there are functioning systems for the distribution of merit, these systems should be used because these merit or promotion committees are in a good position to judge whose departure will least undermine the university's functioning. Dismissals, in such a system, would be based on the lack of merit, not on age. Seniority should only be considered a criterion if one position must be eliminated and there are two candidates for dismissal who are equal in every other respect.

Seniority is vigorously defended by some faculty union leaders as a necessary protection and this reveals the real danger to Canadian universities from faculty unionism. The prime function of a union is to protect its members. Its very beginnings arose out of the need to protect the mass of the workers who were not likely to rise above their working-class status and enter the middle class or become owners. That was and is a vitally necessary function and, in certain instances. the losses caused the system in terms of efficiency and productivity are far outweighed by the substantial benefits that trade unionism brings in terms of protection and economic advancement for the majority. It works well in a factory. But universities are not factories and the majority in a university, like any majority anywhere, is not composed of exceptional people. Certainly there are outstanding scholars and teachers to be found among the leaders of faculty unions and the Canadian Association of University Teachers, and many of these exceptional people led the drive for trade unionism on Canadian university campuses in the mid-1970s. But their masters, the ordinary members who determine faculty union policy with their votes, are not composed of masses of exceptional people. They are usually the university teachers who do not publish so much, teach so well, or display exceptional talent in administration. They are the ones who need the greatest protection. University professors as a group are no different from any other group – carpenters, home domestics, doctors, or lawyers. There are the very good, the very bad, and the great majority who are neither. The rules, however, are usually designed by the great majority primarily for the benefit of the great majority.[5] Thus, seniority as a criterion for layoffs has become increasingly acceptable at Canadian universities while tenure awarded by an arbitrator is tolerated and the disappearance of merit pay is condoned. This is the start of an attack upon the privileges that excellence brings and that it ought to bring if high-quality teaching and scholarship are to be encouraged at Canadian universities. How far will that attack go?

The Senate and the Perils of Democracy

The senate at almost all Canadian universities is the top legislative body in academic and pedagogical matters, but its structure does not allow it to maintain and safeguard standards of excellence among the academic staff or in matters of program. It is too democratic in one sense and not democratic enough in another. It is too easily led by academic administrators and it thrives on compromise, the destroyer of excellence.

Most university senates were reformed along the lines suggested by Duff and Berdahl – election, on a faculty by faculty basis, of the majority of senate – and despite the rise of collective bargaining and faculty unions they remain responsible for academic programs and standards at almost all Canadian universities. The senate sets admission, pass, fail, and graduation requirements for students. The senate lays out curriculum requirements, establishes or gives official approval to honours and graduate programs, and gives final approval to the university calendar, the official document that lays out the university's complete program and regulations. Senates also watch over the quality of the academic staff by setting standards, sometimes on a shared basis with unions for the granting of tenure and the awarding of promotions.

Since the majority of senate members are elected to represent specific faculties, they sit as representatives of the special interests of those faculties. They examine proposed new programs and changes to existing programs from the perspective of protecting their faculty's interests. Like members of a legislature, they engage in compromise and trade-offs in the search for a majority. This is good from a democratic point of view. It virtually ensures, however, that radical improvements to programs or standards that will adversely affect the interests of strong faculties will fail to pass the senate. Senate members representing a science faculty, for example, will not look kindly on a program proposal that might force large numbers of students enrolled in their faculty to take courses in another faculty as part of a degree requirement. Members of all faculties would balk at raising admission and pass standards or setting basic competency requirements – in English composition and spelling, for example – that might cut the number of students attending university because such academic upgrading would adversely affect government funding, usually tied directly to enrolments in one way or another.

Duff and Berdahl recommended that university senates have a majority of academic members and some senates still do. But a surprising number do not, if a recent CAUT survey is any indication. A report on the collegial process in Canadian universities, compiled by the Academic Freedom and Tenure Committee of the Association in the fall of 1983, noted that only nine of twenty-four associations responding to the survey reported that faculty members were in a majority on their senates. This is appalling. It has undoubtedly resulted from the widespread practice of university administrators appointing themselves to senates. When these *ex-officio* representatives are lumped together with student representatives and others, the faculty no longer form a clear majority.

Administrators on senates are there by virtue of their place in the administrative structure and can be expected to support the administration almost automatically. Whatever the policy or approach of the president, they will support it. Sometimes these automatic votes will be used to advance quality and excellence in the program and among the staff, but they will not be so cast because of the intrinsic merits of proposals; they will be cast instead according to the dictates of the administration. The interests of administrators and rank-and-file professors are often different. It is inherently in the interests of the administrators, for example, to have peace between boards and senates and between boards and provincial governments, and here, too, the impulse to compromise and horse-trading is strong. It is not conducive to the improvement of higher education itself. There are too many administration votes on university senates.

There are also too many student votes. Duff and Berdahl made their report before the cancer of student revolt ate away at Canadian campuses in the late 1960s. They anticipated that this might occur – they were not blind to events in the United States and in Europe – and they concluded that students ought to have greater representation in some areas of the university administration. But they did not recommend the wholesale granting of student representation on senates that has since occurred. There was much wisdom in this. Students are directly interested in program and in trying to control faculty. It is human nature, and as fundamental as greed, to want to exercise control over the people who will determine whether you pass or fail, whether you graduate with distinction or just graduate, whether you win scholarships or work your way through university. It is also human nature to try to smooth obstacles and lower barriers.

Student representation is, or can be, a double-edged sword in the battle to re-establish high standards at the university. On the one hand, students will instinctively resist the raising of pass or admission standards because it will make their work more difficult; on the other, they have a direct interest in ensuring that their degree is truly worth something when they graduate. But this conflict should not be allowed to influence decisions on academic standards. There is too much riding on the outcome to gamble that students who support high standards will always have the upper hand in student government and thus on university senates. Recent history shows that this is not the case. During the student revolt days of the 1960s student leaders railed against "bourgeois" standards in universities; in the recent past a more conservative crowd has been less reluctant to admit that there is merit in doing well in a difficult course. When will the swing come once again?

As it now exists at most universities in Canada, senate structure is an impediment to excellence and a stimulant to mediocrity. It is a formidable barrier to improvement of the system because it raises legislative logrolling to an end in itself. Senates should be drastically changed as soon as possible by denying the vote to administrators and students and by making provision for the appointment to the senate of voting members of the academic staff from those who have distinguished themselves in teaching and scholarship. A large block of seats in the senate should be reserved for representatives of the full professor rank appointed by a committee of full professors chosen in some appropriate fashion. This would be a highly elitist move but elitism is sorely needed in the determination of standards for the awarding of tenure and promotion and the designing of academic programs. University democracy serves the cause of democracy, a worthy end, but it does not serve the cause of excellence.

Return to Real Shared Authority

It may be too late to save Canadian universities from the worst malignancies of unionism, especially when a self-interested structure has developed among the leaders of faculty unions, the faculty union professional officers, and the ranks of the Canadian Association of University Teachers, but it is worth a try. Those who have chosen to certify can choose to decertify if such a move would improve their situation. Genuine shared authority would be such an improvement.

The biggest error committed by Duff and Berdahl in their report was their assumption that the faculty and the board could be trusted to find some informal system of salary determination that would not break down under stress. They failed to see that businessmen who dominated boards would, in the crunch, act like businessmen and would treat their faculty members not as equals but as employees. And they failed to see that university teachers, enlightened as they may be, were also self-interested humans who will act to defend themselves when they perceive their positions to be threatened. Thus Duff and Berdahl made little provision for a real equality of status and stature between the board and the faculty in salary matters, and they made no provision for the resolution of impasses over salary discussions and/or negotiations. Collective bargaining, when restricted by statute to money matters, poses no threat to academic standards and does not create the total adversarial relationship that must inevitably grow out of faculty unionism. Universities that seek to offer a better solution than faculty unionism should ensure that boards are not dominated by businessmen, that board members are never allowed to serve more than one term of office, and that a built-in system for resolving salary impasses would govern board-faculty relations over economic issues. Beyond that, boards, faculty associations, and senates should have equal power and responsibility to determine hiring and layoff policy while senates alone, reformed as suggested above, should have total control over all academic issues. The boards, however, should be given a veto over those matters that relate to the raising or spending of university funds. Such a system can be built on the Duff-Berdahl structures that already exist and will go far to removing the cause of faculty discontent.

Universities were once highly elitist institutions. In some societies they still are. It is clear that the Canadian public, professors, and students will no longer tolerate this and that democracy is essential in the administering of universities. But democracy must now be tempered with a strong dose of elitism in the determination of academic policy and, in its trade union guise, democracy must be limited before it homogenizes the teaching staff, undermines programs, and turns universities into glorified high schools. If we continue to allow unfettered majorities to control academic policy and, through their unions, to determine terms and conditions of employment in government-supervised collective agreements, the Canadian university system will rush headlong down the road to hell. Salvation for higher education in Canada lies not in faculty unionism, not in the continued existence of senates structured as they currently are, but in a courageous admission that a strong dose of elitism and genuine shared authority are the best way to run a university.

Notes

[1] *University Government in Canada: Report of a Commission sponsored by the Canadian Association of University Teachers and the Association of Universities and Colleges of Canada* (Toronto: University of Toronto Press, 1966), pp. 7-8.

[2] *Ibid.*, p. 21.

[3] *Ibid.*, p. 22.

[4] B. L. Adell and D. D. Carter, *Collective Bargaining for University Faculty in Canada* (Kingston: Queen's University Industrial Relations Centre, 1972), pp. 54-55.

[5] A concept discussed in Adell and Carter, pp. 82ff.

CHAPTER IV
Studying in the Supermarket

In the fall of 1968 the light of liberty burned briefly inside the large concrete cube of the Henry F. Hall building of Sir George Williams University in downtown Montreal. A student commune composed of a loose coalition of militant blacks, white liberals, and socialist revolutionaries took control of the university's nerve centre – its multi-million dollar computer complex. This collection of student guerillas wielded fire axes as they barricaded themselves inside the computer centre behind piles of smashed furniture. They issued a series of demands, threats, and ultimatums aimed at liberating Sir George from the grip of fascist administrators and racist professors. After a standoff that lasted several days the university authorities authorized the forces of oppression to launch a search-and-destroy mission aimed at retaking the computer centre and restoring the normal repressive order of the institution. A brief but fierce battle raged. The students swung their axes – their hammers of freedom – against the innards of the electronic monsters that represented the evil new technology university administrations used to control and manipulate them. They set fire to their surroundings, showing the world their heroic revolutionary willingness to die among the ruins of their own Stalingrad in the Hall building. They showered the streets of Montreal with computer cards that were not to be punched, stapled, spindled, or folded (thus destroying years of research of professors and graduate students alike, but research undoubtedly aimed at furthering the cause of the Pentagon), and they battled the forces of fascism who broke through the barricades and extinguished the light of revolutionary freedom and student equality that had burned so briefly inside the computer centre. The students lost their fight for liberty but they set a shining example for their oppressed brothers and sisters everywhere.

It didn't really happen that way, of course, except in the fevered minds of a handful of student revolutionaries who seemed to control most of the student press in Canada, who dominated the executives of many student governments, and who led the Canadian Union of Students. It was, when stripped of the phoney revolutionary rhetoric, one of the worst cases of Ludditism that marked the student revolt of the last years of the 1960s. It was an unjustified and criminal assault, not only on the property of the university, but upon the thousands of hours of research and scholarly inquiry that those computer cards, thrown into the streets, represented. It was also an attack on the integrity and courage of university administrators and teaching staff, which stimulated the sheep-like timidity and the willingness to abandon principle of so many who ran Canada's universities in those days of unrest. It was the culmination, the extreme but logical conclusion, of a process that had started several years before in the United States and which eventually spread to Canada – a process that set in motion changes in the structure, philosophy, and integrity of Canadian universities.

The burning of the computer centre at Sir George Williams University was the high point – or low point – in an era of student unrest that touched, in one way or another, almost every campus across the country. Following the example of student radicals in the United States who had started their assault on society in the early 1960s, Canadian students demanded change, sometimes revolutionary change, in almost every aspect of higher education. In the United States students were spurred to action by the drives for black rights and the campaign to get the United States out of Southeast Asia. Led by increasingly militant organizations such as the Student Non-Violent Coordinating Committee and the Students for a Democratic Society, American university and college students stormed the bastions of higher education, occupied and destroyed university property, conducted massive student strikes, held university teachers and administrators hostage, and demanded radical change to admission requirements, curriculum structure, university government, the distribution of university funds, and the basic relationships between students and professors. Hardly a week passed from 1966 to 1970 without some major manifestation of student unrest and violence from one end of the United States to the other. The oppressed student masses, rising against their masters, made common cause with poor blacks, workers, and the people of the Third World. They somehow forgot their pampered middle-class origins, the social and economic advantages that society was handing them on a silver platter, and the scorn, contempt, and cynicism that the real poor and oppressed usually felt for them. No matter, it was a holy crusade. No one over thirty was to be trusted. The last administrator of the last university was to be hanged with the entrails of the last capitalist whose oppressive system the universities supported.

It was inevitable that the student revolt would cross the borders into Canada. It came in the intellectual baggage of American draft evaders convinced by the Fords on the streets, the Coca-Cola signs on the highways, and "Laugh-In" on the tube that Canada was just a smaller, more staid version of the U.S. And it was imported by Canadian student radicals who had no Vietnam War to protest against and no South in which to conduct voter registration drives. The rhetoric and the action soon heated up. The campuses had to be burned in order to be saved, student leaders shouted. The "Student as Nigger" – an absurdist phrase of the period – had to break the chains of oppression, wrote the editors of the miniature *Pravdas* that passed for the student press around the country. And the student revolt, Canadian edition, was soon underway. Here, as in the U.S., demonstrations, sit-ins, and occupations became all the rage. And here, too, misguided professors and administrators, some suffering a mere lack of courage, others seeking allies for their own revolutionary ambitions, still others trying to recapture their lost youth, aided and abetted the radicals at worst or, at best, took no firm or resolute action to stop them. It all culminated at Sir George Williams University in the fall of 1968. When the police and firemen of the city of Montreal finally took back the computer centre, the party had ended, and the long hangover began to set in. We are living with it still.

The destruction of the computer centre at Sir George was a tragedy. Property was destroyed and lives were disrupted. But the computers were replaced, the research projects eventually salvaged, and the students who were duped by the revolutionary leaders eventually came to their senses, for the most part. This was not the greatest damage the student revolt caused on Canadian campuses. The real damage, the long-run underlying damage, was far more serious and has proven far more permanent. In the frenzy of changing things for the sake of meeting student demands, universities across Canada altered admission and curriculum requirements, watered down or eliminated core requirements, began a steady grade inflation, and introduced the misguided and damaging concept that students were entitled to the same treatment, the same privileges, and the same right to determine the course of university government as professors. The result has been a dangerous erosion of the quality and value of the education students are receiving at Canadian universities and the granting of degrees to people who should not hold them.

Taking the Guards from the Gates

It is an axiom that anything worthwhile is difficult to get. That is why banks put money in vaults. It is no trick to get hold of things that have no value and that, of course, is what makes them valueless. So, too, with a university education. It was once difficult to achieve the academic qualifications to enter a Canadian university, but it is difficult no more. At present (although there are signs of change) it is still almost true that anyone who wants to enter a Canadian university and embark on the pursuit of a degree can do so. This is so not only because of the changes made to entrance requirements by universities in the great panic to "liberalize" caused by the student revolt of the 1960s, but also, as we have seen, because of government policies and the greed of university administrators and professors. Provincial governments, using their own funds and funds passed to them from the federal government, created systems of university financing that were usually tied to the number of warm and functioning student bodies on campus. The more student flesh, the higher the annual grant. Universities, eager to expand plant and equipment, add new staff, and buy more books and computers, grabbed the money and ran. It served no one's purpose to maintain high entrance requirements because they clearly meant fewer students, and fewer students meant fewer dollars.

This move to lower entrance standards came just at the time that most provincial departments of education, in their infinite wisdom, began to abolish departmental or matriculation examinations as the prime means by which high school students were tested prior to graduation. It was once thought that the true measure of what a student had learned in high school could only be gained by impartial examinations, set by provincial authorities, and graded anonymously at the end of a student's career in high school. The theory was based on the assumption that a classroom teacher might be more lenient toward his charges after sharing a classroom with them for ten months and knowing that future education progress depended on the results of a final examination. The system was, however, increasingly cumbersome and expensive to operate as the surging baby boom enrolments multiplied graduating classes and, at the same time, the experts concluded that there were surely better ways of measuring what a student had learned in high school than a one shot, "winner take all" departmental examination. So, slowly but surely, from one end of the country to the other, departmental and matriculation examinations were abolished, and the classroom teacher was given the authority to determine the final grades of students leaving high school. And sure enough, a wholesale inflation of high school leaving grades began. It has not ended yet. Students taking basic English and mathematics examinations during their first year at university have been failing *en masse* for the last half decade. A study conducted at the University of Calgary has revealed that high school graduates attending the university in the mid-1970s fared worse than graduates with the same high school grades at the end of the 1960s. Some high school teachers have gone to great lengths to deny that this erosion has taken place. It is a self-serving argument that flies in the face of mounting evidence. It is no wonder that provincial departments of education across Canada are beginning to take another look at departmental and matriculation examinations.

Universities naturally relied heavily on departmental and matriculation examination grades in setting standards for admission. They trusted those grades and, for the most part, those grades did provide a fair measure on an across-province basis of a student's ability. But they were not the only measure used. Many Canadian universities acknowledged that Johnny or Sally might have had the potential to gain a university degree but had not "bloomed" in high school, and they added entrance examinations of their own or required students to sit for competency examinations established by institutions such as the College Entrance Examination Board in the United States. Some universities also asked for letters of reference from high school teachers, principals, or other community members who were thought to be in a position to judge the potential student. There were, therefore, many hurdles. Most high school graduates did not get into universities and those who did were generally qualified to attempt the first-year course of study.

By the end of the 1960s this had changed radically. Universities stopped their own testing (it was expensive and time-consuming), dropped the requirement to sit for general competency examinations such as those set by the CEEB (it was an American body), and lowered the grade requirement for admission. Today most Canadian universities require a high school graduation certificate, an average grade of 60 to 65 per cent, and a bare pass on a certain number of required courses. These grades are awarded by classroom teachers. Grade inflation among high school graduates and easier entrance requirements set by universities have taken the guards from the gates. At this point virtually anyone who graduates from high school is eligible to attend university or, even if rejected, can usually gain entrance as a "mature" student a few years later. This was certainly not always true. One dramatic result of this began to show up several years ago at a number of campuses across the country when first-year students sat for English-language competence examinations. In the late 1970s, as complaints began to flood university administrators from businesses, professional schools, and even school boards that university graduates could barely read, write, or spell, universities began to set exams to test the literacy of first-year students. The results were appalling – from one end of Canada to the other, students failed these exams at a rate that was usually close to 50 per cent. In some cases students who had graduated from high school English courses with excellent grades were found to be unable to write. Few of them, after all, had ever had to prepare an essay.

Today, Canadian universities let almost everyone in who wants to get in. Some people applaud that as an example of the liberalization of access to higher education. Perhaps it is a good thing to allow such free access. But the problem is that few are allowed to fail. In the French university system, there is almost total access the first year. There is, however, a very high failure rate of students trying to pass to second year. The philosophy is to let everyone in and then weed out the less able. This is one approach to accessibility. Many Canadian medical schools take the opposite approach. Their entrance requirements are so high that virtually no one fails who gains admittance. The students who get in are very good and the staff has so much faith in their admission requirements that if something does go wrong with a student, there is generally a way of setting the student straight and ensuring success. When it comes to access to the undergraduate program at most Canadian universities, however, we have the worst of both worlds. Almost everyone gets in and almost everyone passes.

There are some signs of change in the air. Under the pressure of the increased enrolments of the early 1980s and frozen government funding, many Canadian universities are more crowded than they have ever been. Students continue to enrol but there are no funds for more teachers, classrooms, or labs. The quality of education is declining even more. The once sacrilegious thought that students should compete for a limited number of openings in first year is now regaining ground. The University of British Columbia announced, in early 1984, that only the top 3,250 applicants would be admitted regardless of how many students meet the basic admission requirements. A similar scheme is under study at the University of Calgary, and some Ontario universities are also moving in this direction. But these are still voices crying in the wilderness. For the moment, at most universities, there are virtually no guards at the gates.

Oh, For Bo-Bo English!

Almost every university in Canada once had a "Bo-Bo" English course. That was the English literature course specially designed for engineering students. Registrars and senates reasoned that engineers had little capacity for Shakespeare after destroying millions of brain cells with heavy drinking and wearing out the balance on complex math. They made allowance for this with Bo-Bo English, a watered-down version of the compulsory English literature course at the heart of the core curriculum all undergraduates were forced to complete. Bo-Bo English was easier, less exhaustive, and perhaps more suitable for the underdeveloped literary lobes of engineers; but it was compulsory. The university, in those days, believed that every student who graduated should have some knowledge of the English literary tradition and the religious, philosophical, and cultural values that go with it and form the foundation of our society. The university also ensured in passing that students could at least write their way out of a wet paper bag, even if they were not capable of breathless flights of fancy prose. Today, for the most part, Bo-Bo English is gone. Compulsory courses of any sort are gone. The core curriculum is gone. The supermarket is here.

The basic core curriculum that was once a universal part of higher education was designed to ensure that every student completing university had acquired the basic requirements of a liberal arts education. Engineering, English, and economics majors were all forced by strict degree requirements to study a number of specific subjects that introduced the student to a core of knowledge. The requirements of the core curriculum differed from campus to campus but it was taken for granted almost everywhere. It usually forced the first-year student in particular to take courses in English literature, mathematics, and science whatever the eventual area of specialization that student selected. There was often little free choice for these students and even options could only be chosen from specified areas. A student might, therefore, aim at a B.Sc. with honours in chemistry but in first-year study English literature, an introduction to philosophy, history, and even a foreign language in addition to chemistry, physics, or mathematics. There was more freedom of choice in second year, and more concentration in subjects touching directly on chemistry, but here, too, a student was usually compelled to take courses outside the area of specialization. The last two years of the degree program were usually, but not always, filled with the honours specialization courses.

The core curriculum that once existed almost everywhere in Canadian universities evolved from the even tighter curriculum requirements of the previous generation. In the 1920s and 1930s universities and colleges existed primarily as liberal arts institutions training young men and women how to think. Knowledge, of the kind we now style technical or professional, was to be acquired after the first degree was earned in schools that taught medicine, engineering, or the law. The old undergraduate programs were heavily loaded with literature, philosophy, the classics, languages, mathematics, and traditional disciplines such as history and economics. This kind of curriculum had started to disappear in the decades after World War Two and was killed in the 1960s. The flood of warm bodies into the universities, the student revolt, and the demands of governments that universities teach "useful" things created a revolution that wiped away the philosophy that students should be taught how to think and substituted the belief that they should be taught how to do. That, at first glance, looks like a change for the better – we now get more knowledge for the dollar. Perhaps so. But we also get a large number of ignorant university graduates who hide their ignorance behind the specialized titles of their chosen profession. And we get a less humane society at the same time.

Honours: Tunnels to Specialized Ignorance

In the last two decades universities across Canada have been pushing the specialized honours degree that allows little room for students to learn anything except that area in which they choose to specialize. Students who graduate with such degrees know more and more about less and less, contributing to the excessive specialization and narrowness of society as a whole.

Every day we face the consequences of our specialized ignorance. Traffic planners wanting to push freeways or rapid transit systems through neighbourhoods usually have little or no knowledge of family structure, local economic development, or neighbourhood cultural values. Oil companies wishing to build deep-water oil ports often fail to see the impact on the ecosystem or the possible effects on the local economy. We are now more aware of our need for integrated knowledge and we are trying harder with the tools we have to approach these sorts of problems from an integrated perspective. But the tools and the knowledge we have are often faulty, in part because of the system of higher education. We expect doctors to make decisions about abortion and euthanasia but we do not force them to study philosophy, religion, sociology, or history to show them how such powers were used or abused in the past, the religious and moral implications of their actions, or the implications of their decisions for the future of humankind. So doctors, like lawyers, engineers, accountants, and other professionals, are increasingly becoming the hired gunfighters of our society, ready to do our bidding with less and less thought as to the social or moral implications of their actions. These are the results of overspecialization in our educational system and of the failure of universities to educate students to think for themselves and to be aware of the broad foundations of wisdom upon which our civilization is based.

Students entering university today choose between general and honours programs. The general programs have been stigmatized as catch-alls for the unworthy. Those with low grades and those who are unable or unwilling at the ripe age of eighteen to map out careers are encouraged to enter the general programs. The general B.A. or B.Sc. is usually a three-year program and students are not ordinarily required to specialize in specific areas such as biology or sociology. They are, however, forced to take almost all of their courses within one faculty. A general B.A. student would find it impossible, for example, to take a large number of science courses at any Canadian university.

In the honours program, students usually follow a four-year regimen, entering the honours program at the end of the first year. At Concordia University, for example, a student honouring in biology would take a sequence of courses approved by the departmental honours adviser in biology, chemistry, zoology, botany, ecology, and cell and molecular biology. At least seventy-two out of the ninety credits required for the honours degree must fall within this program. At Carleton University a student honouring in political science is required to take at least nine credits in political science alone out of the twenty required for the degree. This is a somewhat more flexible program than the biology honours program at Concordia but it is still too heavily concentrated. The majority of honours programs at Canadian universities fall somewhere in between these two limits. The result is the same – great, even extreme, specialization within one area.

Honours programs are generally designed by the department concerned. Within universities departments are engaged in a constant struggle for the funds allocated by the university's central budget authority to each faculty and within each faculty to each department. The pie is constant, but the size of the slice is ordinarily decided by using complex formulas that are supposed to determine which departments teach the greatest number of students. Departments are aware of this and aware also that changing the number of sections offered in each course, adding or deleting courses, labs, and tutorials, and changing course requirements can all affect the figures. Two different departments with the same number of faculty members and teaching the same number of students can show two very different profiles to faculty or university budget committees. Depending on how courses and course sections are organized, one department may look drastically overworked while the other presents a picture of overpaid, underworked teachers with little or nothing to do. This promotes diddling of the figures – and what better way to diddle figures than to force honours students to sup almost exclusively from the departmental trough? There is, then, little danger they will take courses from other departments and lower the number of weekly student contact hours – a key measure of faculty workload and the department's need for funds.

Honours programs are designed to force students to follow a highly specialized regimen and to maintain a high grade average in the core subject. They are elitist by nature, but they are necessary if university students are to begin to grasp highly complex subjects such as nuclear physics or molecular biology. They must not be scrapped; but they have become too specialized and should be modified so that they are not as highly concentrated as they are now and students are not required to enter them so early. And yet, in the halcyon days of student revolt the University of Toronto went to the other extreme and abolished honours programs outright and substituted "specialist" programs instead. Here was elitism turned on its head; the intellectuals, in the best Maoist tradition, were forced to work in the fields alongside the peasants. The result was not only the undermining of the once high standards of honours undergraduate education at the university but a consequent lowering of student morale.

The Supermarket Curriculum

Today there is little left of the core curriculum that first- and second-year students were once forced to take. At the University of British Columbia, all first-year B.A. students are required to take English 100, a combination literature and English composition course. The requirement was brought in recently when the university learned, to its horror, that the high school students it was admitting seemed to be functionally illiterate. First-year students are also required to take "one full course in science" – it is not specified that this include laboratory time (there is no better way to learn about the scientific method than doing labs) – and a full course in literature, usually in second year. They must prove competence in a language other than English, a very tough requirement in this permissive age. The closest program to this is at the University of Ottawa, where students working toward a general B.A. degree are required to take certain English literature and composition courses and a course in philosophy.

These programs, as weak as they are, are the exception; most Canadian universities have adopted the "area" approach to setting course requirements. First-year students aiming at a B.Sc. at the University of Alberta are told to take three science courses, one arts course, and one open option. B.A. students at the University of Calgary are required to choose ten half-courses spread out over four subject areas, with the bulk of their courses in the humanities and social sciences. At Dalhousie University, students are given four subject areas to choose from – sciences, social sciences, humanities, and languages – and in first year are told to take at least one course from each area with no more than two in one subject and one "selected from a list ... in which written work is considered frequently and in detail." These requirements are typical of those at other Canadian universities.

The intention, at first glance, looks honourable. Students have to acquaint themselves with different subjects and disciplines before deciding their areas of specialization. But this is a far different thing from a core curriculum. In the majority of Canadian universities, students are not required to take any specific subject; the calendar treats all subjects the same, as if they were of equal importance. There is no prescribed routine and students, in their great wisdom, are given almost total freedom to choose courses. Few are up to the task of choosing wisely.

In some universities students are not required to take any courses outside their disciplinary area at all. At the University of Ottawa, for example, one of the few institutions to offer anything like a core program for general B.A. students, no science course of any kind is required. At the University of Toronto a similar situation exists. At the University of New Brunswick, first-year students are told to choose their courses from at least three of the four subject areas, roughly corresponding to languages, humanities, social sciences, and sciences. Nor is there a science requirement at UNB at the second- and upper-year levels. And this, though an extreme case, is indicative of the problem.

All these programs are based on the assumption that students should have the freedom to choose. But why should they have such freedom? Few first-year students have the knowledge or experience to choose the sort of program that would give them a solid foundation of essential knowledge. Like kids in a candy store they will usually grab at the brightest baubles – or the easiest courses. We are allowing university students to equip themselves with the knowledge tools of their own choosing instead of forcing them to acquire a set of skills that others, more experienced and more knowledgeable, know are necessary. Such a system does not offer freedom, it gives licence. Some students may choose wisely, but society can no longer afford to gamble on the wisdom of nineteen-year-olds, especially when taxpayers are footing more than 75 per cent of the university bill. It was irresponsible for universities to grant this much freedom in the first place; it is time for a return to sanity.

A core curriculum is built on the assumption that there is a body of knowledge to which all educated persons in society should be introduced, that some subjects are more important than others, and that students should be introduced to those subjects in a logical and orderly fashion. Several years ago, the Council of Harvard University's Faculty of Arts and Science approved the introduction of a new core curriculum for its undergraduate program. The move came after the issuance of a report ("Undergraduate Education: Defining the Issues") that outlined basic principles for undergraduate education in the university of today. They are worth repeating because they can be applied as well to Canada as to the United States:

1) An educated person must be able to think and write clearly and effectively.

2) An educated person should have a critical appreciation of the ways in which we gain knowledge and understanding of the universe, of society and of ourselves. Specifically, he or she should have an informed acquaintance with the aesthetic and intellectual experience of literature and the arts; with history as a mode of understanding present problems and the processes of human affairs; with the concepts and analytic techniques of modern social science; with philosophical analysis, especially as it relates to the moral dilemmas of modern men and women; and with the mathematical and experimental methods of the physical and biological sciences.

3) An educated American, in the last third of this century, cannot be provincial in the sense of being ignorant of other cultures and other times. It is no longer possible to conduct our lives without reference to the wider world within which we live. A crucial difference between the educated and the uneducated is the extent to which one's life experience is viewed in wider contexts.

4) An educated person is expected to have some understanding of, and experience in thinking about, moral and ethical problems. It may well be that the most significant quality in educated persons is the informed judgment which enables them to make discriminating moral choices.

5) Finally, an educated individual should have achieved depth in some field of knowledge. Cumulative learning is an effective way to develop a student's powers of reasoning and analysis, and for our undergraduates this is the principal role of concentrations.

The Harvard core curriculum was founded on the recognition of two basic ideas: the need to introduce students to broader knowledge and wisdom than previously and the recognition that specialization has a legitimate and even vital part to play in a university education.

We do not bow before the name "Harvard." It is far from a perfect institution and even there faculty still give, and students still take, "Mickey Mouse" courses that allow students to increase their grades with little effort. At that august university knowledge and the process of its acquisition are still highly specialized and curriculum reform has been a long process. The statement of principles, however, loses none of its validity despite Harvard's imperfections; it should light the way to change like a shining beacon. But it does not. It was issued more than eight years ago and has passed virtually unnoticed in Canada. Instead, Canadian universities have gone the opposite way: they genuflect, in the first year and in some general degree programs, toward universality, but without imposing any order or direction on the pursuit of this general knowledge. Then they quickly ram students into highly concentrated and inflexible honours programs with extreme specialization.

Goring Oxen

There are formidable obstacles to the introduction, or re-introduction, of core curricula programs at Canadian universities. It is not that people deny the intrinsic merit of such programs – most professors and administrators would, if asked, acknowledge the wisdom of the Harvard statement of principles. At the same time, however, they would consider it naive, idealistic, and impossible to achieve given the reality of Canadian universities. There are two major sets of obstacles: the structure of the institutions and the composition of the governing bodies that are responsible for curricula.

Few universities today contain a Faculty of Arts and Science. Almost all Canadian universities have split Arts and Science into separate faculties and a few – Calgary, Carleton, and the University of Western Ontario are good examples – have created three where once there was one. Now there are two or three deans instead of one, two or three faculty budgets, and two or three sets of faculty committees to allocate funds, design curricula requirements, and perform other functions. It also means that now two or three faculties are struggling against each other for funds at the university level and attempting to hoard as many students as possible, thus proving the need for the greatest share of the budget pie. In some instances faculties go to extreme lengths to keep students in the fold. They are beginning to offer courses that might naturally be offered in other faculties on the justification that such courses are necessary to the program when, in fact, they are bald efforts to keep students confined within the paper walls of faculty requirements. The construction of a core program that could meet the objectives outlined by Harvard for its undergraduate students cannot be carried out under such circumstances. There are too many jealousies and rivalries. More faculties than ever are now competing for fewer dollars and there is little chance that the members of one faculty will encourage students from that faculty to take core courses elsewhere. The budgeting process is, therefore, a major obstacle to the building of a core curriculum.

So is the nature of university government. Most Canadian university senates are supposed to represent the interests of faculty members, administrators, and students and are charged with the power to set admission requirements, establish new programs, set up or abolish courses, and generally govern the academic side of the university. Faculties are represented on these bodies in numbers corresponding to faculty size by elected representatives. There are too many oxen to be gored for university senates, as they are now structured, to introduce core curricula. A core program built on the assumption that some areas of knowledge are more important than others would run into heavy going in a university senate from those faculties whose courses would be excluded from the core program. Students, who now have heavy representation on university senates, could be expected to oppose the introduction of core curricula because such programs will restrict their freedom of action and make university more difficult. Given the current structure of university budgeting and government there is little chance that Canadian universities will decide to return to the serious business of teaching students how to think, introducing them to basic areas of knowledge, and forcing them to complete pre-determined requirements before they rush headlong into the tunnel of specialization that the honours programs have become.

Stay Alive, Get an 'A'

Students still fail at Canadian universities, but not as much as they used to, and they get A and B grades far more frequently than they did in the past. We not only let more students into university who are not truly qualified, we let more of them pass and give a larger number of them better grades. A student who graduates with a B average today would likely have received a C+ twenty years ago. (Teachers, amusingly enough, point to this phenomenon to prove that the new grading system turns out better students.) Professors and university administrators love to point self-righteously to the grade inflation that has undermined the value of a high school education, but they are themselves guilty of causing or acquiescing in a grade inflation in the universities that is steadily eroding the real value of a university degree.

Once upon a time, there was the bell curve. It was a guide to the distribution of grades at universities and was based on the axiom that few of us are outstanding, few of us are very poor, and the great bulk of us lie somewhere in between. If a bell curve is applied to the performance of students in a given class, a small number of students at the very top will be awarded A grades and a small (but somewhat larger) number at the bottom of the class will fail. The majority will earn a grade slightly better than C. It was and is a patently unfair system of grading because students who deserve high grades on the basis of their actual performance in a class may not receive those grades if there are too many excellent students in one class and students who should be failed may not be failed if there are too many poor students. In its heyday it was applied rigorously in some classes (usually science courses where a large number of multiple choice exams were and are used) and totally ignored in others. Even though it is an unfair system, however, it serves as a constant reminder to the professor that all students are not as excellent as others, and it forces professors to protect the value of higher grades. Students who constantly receive A grades under a bell curve system are truly and without question the best of their class. The bell curve ensured that grading standards remained the same from year to year; if a professor was unduly harsh in grading in one year and very generous in the next, the same percentage of A grades would emerge from the class.

The bell curve is gone (good riddance!) but nothing has replaced it. From year to year average grades awarded at Canadian universities creep higher and higher. Figures to prove this are almost impossible to obtain from universities – they are aware that grade inflation is a serious matter and do not want to draw attention to it – but statistics are available from the University of Calgary and the University of Alberta, and these are disturbing indeed. At the University of Calgary grades awarded across the university in 1982 were almost 22 per cent higher in 1982 than in 1969! At the University of Alberta there has been almost no grade inflation across the university as a whole since 1970 – the average grade there was a generous B or better even then – but there has been significant inflation in faculties such as Business and especially in upper-level courses. At both universities it is clear that some faculties and disciplines are now awarding high grades far more frequently than they did a decade and a half ago.

The University of Alberta uses a unique nine-point grade system that makes direct comparison with other universities somewhat difficult. We shall, therefore, examine the statistics from the University of Calgary, which uses the almost universal grade point average system based on 4. In this system an A grade is worth 4, a B grade is worth 3, a C grade is worth 2, and a D is worth 1. Thus, a student who achieves three A's, a B, and a C in a given year has earned 17 points for an average of 3.66 or B+. In 1969 the average grade awarded at the University of Calgary was 2.41 or C+, but by 1982 that average had climbed to 2.59 or B–. In some faculties (Social Science and Social Welfare) the average grade awarded in 1982 was a B, which strains credibility. At the same time the number of students receiving failing grades in some U. of C. faculties has dropped to the point where the F has become almost obsolete. In 1982 only 3 per cent of the grades awarded in the Faculty of Science were F grades, while only 2 per cent of the grades awarded in the Faculty of Social Science were F. It may be argued that few F grades are awarded because student withdrawals are on the increase (allowing them to avoid failing) but the statistics do not support this. Withdrawals have remained almost constant in the whole university over the past decade and have declined in Science and Social Science. There can only be two explanations for these statistics: students are getting better or professors are becoming more generous. However, there is mounting evidence that high school graduates are not as good as they once were and that they have benefited from grade inflation at the secondary level. These same students, then, must also be benefiting from grade inflation at university. Besides, even if students are better prepared for university today than they were ten years ago, which is doubtful, they should surely be judged by the same standards as students were ten years ago and should be matched against each other in the same way. In fact, the Faculty of Engineering at the University of Calgary has been remarkably consistent in how it has awarded grades over the past decade and there has been no grade inflation at all. Does this mean that engineering students are getting poorer in comparison to other students? Does it mean that other students are getting brighter? Or does it mean that the professors at the Faculty of Engineering are as rigorous in grading today as they were a decade ago? All the available evidence, and common sense, points to the last conclusion as being closest to the truth.

**Equality Breeds Familiarity,
Familiarity Breeds Contempt**

The prime cause of grade inflation in universities today is familiarity – in many classes (and this is more pronounced in some disciplines than in others) students and professor have become buddies. Students are accepted as equals in the classroom, in the common room, on university committees, and on governing bodies. This grew directly out of the student revolts of the late 1960s and reversed the age-old relationship between the student who came to learn and the professor who was there to teach and assess performance. That simple relationship is no longer accepted as a basic operating principle in Canadian universities.

The clearest evidence of this, and perhaps the one factor that has contributed most to grade inflation, is student evaluation of teaching. In their mania to quantify professorial performance, administrations at many Canadian universities demand annual evaluations of professorial teaching performance. This evaluation is done in a number of ways: by the head or chairman sitting in the classroom or lecture hall; by one or more professorial peers doing the same; or by students filling in computerized evaluation forms. In addition to these administration evaluations, many student unions perform evaluations of their own and publish the results of those evaluations in course "guides" or "anti-calendars." The whole process is based on the mistaken idea that students are capable of evaluating their professors. Of course, on one level, this is easy: Professor Smith may be an Oscar-winning performer and students know what they like. Smith tells great jokes, shares "life experiences" with students, assigns text books that are not too difficult, and does his best to entertain as well as lecture. Students can and do measure these factors. But if Professor Smith is a hard marker, giving few A grades and lots of C and D grades, the student evaluation will always reflect this: students don't like low marks. But students, as persons who come to learn, don't know whether Professor Smith knows what he is talking about when he teaches. They can't know whether his lectures are complete or not or whether he is adequately covering the course. They cannot know because they have come to learn and, therefore, are not in a position to judge. Yet judge they do, with the active connivance of the administration. So when the time comes for Professor Smith to be considered for promotion it pays him to have buddied up to the students, to have graded generously, and to have scored high on his teaching evaluations.

The teaching evaluation is only one piece of evidence of the equality that students have achieved at the university, an equality that is undeserved and which undermines the academic rigour of the institution. Students demanded this equality, and they were given it by professors and administrators in the late 1960s because they claimed they had a right to help determine the shape and course of the institution that was shaping their own lives. It was an irresistible argument in those days of democracy run wild in higher education. But universities are closest to elementary and secondary schools in what they do, and no one has ever suggested that high school students are, or should be, equal to teachers and principals in running the high schools any more than novitiates should have the right to determine the future of the monastery.

Student equality is now a rule of life at all levels of the university. Students are represented on boards of governors. They hold a large number of seats on university senates. They are represented on university grants committees, budget committees, program committees. They hold positions on faculty-staff affairs committees and on departmental promotion and tenure committees. This varies from institution to institution but student participation is now the rule, not the exception. Explanations must be proffered for the absence of students on university committees, not their participation.

And this has also found its way into the classroom. Many professors now have the attitude that the opinion of the students is just as valuable as their own opinion. They discuss, they commiserate, they rap. They do not *teach*. The idea that uninformed opinion is *not* valuable is now heresy.

The classroom, as a teaching place, must be an arena in which discussion is allowed, in which questions are asked and answered, in which students can freely challenge the opinions of professors. Such challenges, after all, help guard academic freedom in that they help ensure that professors present a fair view, and not just their own view, of the subject matter they are teaching. But it must be clear in the classroom, as well as in the university committees and the university government, that student opinion, even coming from articulate, intelligent, and sincere students, is still unformed, rough, and usually without the benefit of extensive knowledge and experience. If it were otherwise, the students would be standing at the podium, not the professor. If a university professor has come to his position by virtue of achieving those standards of scholarship and knowledge that have satisfied his peers of his entitlement to enter the profession (and sometimes this is sadly not the case), then that professor should teach and the students should learn.

Students do not have the knowledge or the experience to determine who should or should not receive tenure or promotion. They are too self-interested to be given a role in deciding the course of study or establishing grade standards. They are too transitory to be given a share in making decisions about long-range programs, budgeting, or staffing. And yet they have a share in making such decisions at universities all across the country. Students should be given influence in decisions of a non-academic nature that affect them – housing, the running of the student union, the operation of extracurricular programs – and they should continue to enjoy full self-government in the affairs of student unions and student government. But that is all. The all-pervasive student influence that exists today should be terminated. Democracy is a fine thing, but too much democracy is anarchy. And although there is no longer the anarchy on university campuses that existed during the days of the student revolt, students have been allowed to keep the gains they won while holding the university to ransom. As long as students vote and have influence on university governing bodies at all levels, they will try their best to keep the university functioning smoothly – as a supermarket run for the consumers' benefit alone.

CHAPTER V

Tenure Is a Four-Letter Word

Tenure is a four-letter word. The public and the press look at the concept and ask, "Why should that S.O.B. have a guaranteed job when I can be laid off whenever the economy goes sour or if I fail to perform?" And, even though most of the public's complaints are directed at public servants employed in the federal bureaucracy or in the provincial capitals, nonetheless university professors catch some of the flak, too.

Our neighbours, for example, have only a very imprecise knowledge of what professors do. They know that we have to go out to the university to lecture or to lead seminars, but that understanding has become almost immaterial to them. What they see is that we are home far more than they are. "Have the year off again?," they say, when we stagger outside for a breath of smog after a day hunched over the typewriter, or when we reel back home after a day spent vainly trying to penetrate the grammatical mistakes in student essays in search of a single, stray idea. In our cases, and in the cases of many of our colleagues, the public perception that professors enjoy a life of indolence, ease, and high salaries is incorrect.

But in many cases, our neighbours' assessment of the situation is all too true. Indolence, ease, and high salaries are in the university, and many of those who enjoy the perquisites of the university have long ago ceased doing anything to earn them. And those professors are protected by tenure. They can only be fired if their university administrations nerve themselves up to a long, bruising battle and charge incompetence. The administration has to be able to prove it and make it stick, quite possibly in a court of law. It will have to fight the university faculty association and, possibly, the Canadian Association of University Teachers, which, while they will know that George is a clod, will see his case as a precedent, a devious plot by the administration that, they fear, is trying to eliminate the entire Philosophy Department or to undermine graduate teaching in George's specialty. Nothing, not even incompetence, in other words, is ever simple in the university context. And after vainly battering their heads against academic obfuscation, most administrations – and most faculty members, who might wish to see their institutions strengthened by the sacking of the dull and their replacement by the able – subside into the muttering of oaths and imprecations. "It's tenure, bloody tenure," they say. "We're powerless." And so they are.

What Is Tenure?

The Canadian Association of University Teachers, the umbrella organization of Canada's university professors, defines tenure as "an appointment without term, which may be terminated only through resignation, retirement or dismissal for good reasons as established by a proper hearing." There can be no doubt that such a secure position is a precious thing in an age of uncertainty. Tenure is also enjoyed by judges, in theory so that they can offer their decisions without fear of political and other pressures. It is enjoyed by civil servants so they can be sure of their posts even if a political party of another persuasion comes into power. But few others have it yet.

In the universities, tenure is achieved after a process of inquiry into a faculty member's abilities. Ordinarily, new faculty are hired for a probationary period, usually up to five years. During that testing time, the faculty members teach, serve on committees, and begin to do the first serious research of their careers outside of graduate school. With luck, they can publish a book (almost always their doctoral dissertation in a revised form), a number of articles (usually chapters spun off from the same dissertation), and if they know someone at a scholarly journal in their discipline, a book review or two (again, likely on subjects closely related to their dissertation subject). This is called "making it," and ordinarily such a process leads to tenure.

The decision to award tenure usually is taken seriously. In most universities, departmental committees are set up to consider George's case. Colleagues are sent into his classroom to watch him instruct his students. Letters are solicited from those who served on committees with him. ("George was extremely diligent on the Parking Committee," such letters might begin. "He attended two of the twelve meetings and was awake for all the votes.") And the young professor's scholarship is appraised. The usual practice is to consider tenure on this three-track system of teaching, service, and scholarship, but different universities put different weight on different components.

The best universities put most weight on scholarship. This may come as a surprise to outsiders who are, like many students, prone to consider good teaching as the be-all and end-all of university work. It's not. In a university context, unlike that of a public school, high school, or community college, good teaching is only possible if it is intimately connected to research. The university, by definition, is a research-oriented institution dedicated to the advance of knowledge, and the best teachers are those who are excited by their own digging into the sources or their work in the laboratory or the field and who can convey their enthusiasm (and suggest promising subjects) to their students. Teaching without research to back it up is often mere showmanship, and too many students, regrettably, snatched away from the television set or the game arcade for a few hours each day, want only to be entertained in the classroom.

That is why the good universities stress scholarship. But in tenure decisions there are always problems in judging quality. Knowledge has many divisions, and a professor of medieval history is not readily able to assess the work of a specialist in Canadian social history, let alone the efforts of a behavioural psychologist. In addition, when academics publish and review books, they denounce each other's errors with great glee. This leads to schools – or cliques, as some might call them – and to cabals; it can also lead to unfairness.

In such circumstances, some tenure committees have been known to throw up their hands in horror. Others, particularly those at weak universities, sometimes tend to say that teaching is more important than what they see as the mindless effort to publish worthless material in vast quantity; still others tend to give great weight to service. After all, these latter committees reason, we are all stuck here in the boondocks, so we had better make sure that the Faculty Club Committee gets a barman who can mix a good Sazerac. What else matters? Sometimes, particularly in those universities where few publish, the work of the few active researchers and writers is scrutinized to death, pored over line by line, its every entrail poked and prodded. To go into print in such institutions is to threaten everyone else, to demonstrate an unhealthy zeal. No tenure for them.

In other words, despite a structure that is designed to ensure fairness, tenure is a decision that can be based on bias, prejudice, professional feuding, simple malice, or local peculiarities. Times change, however, and attitudes change with them. In the early 1970s virtually everyone received tenure; today, with hundreds of young Ph.D.s on the job market, the decision is made carefully and slowly. Such a change in response to market considerations offends many. What should be in place, they insist, is "temporal equity"; treat everyone now the same way we were treated a decade ago. That is an interesting idea and doubtless it is fair; unfortunately, it is a sure recipe for preserving universities in their present awfulness.

Ordinarily the department is the locus where tenure decisions are fought out. Virtually every university has at least one additional review stage where faculty members, sometimes the senior and the distinguished who have been appointed or the junior and unknown who have been elected, appraise the work done by departmental committees. At the over-administered universities, there is a three-stage process that sees a department pass its recommendations up to a faculty (of Arts or Science, e.g.) committee, and then on to a senate committee. Some universities add yet another layer (incredible as it may seem) in the form of a tenure appeals committee. The entire process can take a year or more to work out before the university president gets to see the file and before the board of governors puts its seal of approval on newly tenured Professor George.

Academic Freedom

But what if the board of governors, usually composed of local businessmen, industrialists, and prominenti, decides that George is a shit-disturber, the well-known troublemaker who tried to prevent the construction of an expressway from levelling the homes of the workers? Or that he is a Marxist who is seeking to subvert the established order? Or that his behavioural psychology class treats rats and mice in a cruel and inhuman way? What happens when tenure is denied?

What happens in most cases is that the faculty member had better seek another line of work. If he cannot use the system to protect himself against such interference with his free speech, his research methods, or his off-campus activities, George will be unlikely to get tenure. Most universities are not geared to protect the probationary faculty member against such interference. But they are set up to protect the tenured faculty's right to pursue its work in its own way.

A good thing, too. Tenure originally was designed, as the CAUT says, "to protect free criticism and independent judgment in the interest of the university community and of society at large." That is what tenure is all about. The CAUT "Primer on Tenure" makes the point that "it is eminently in the interests of society that men concerned speak their minds without fear of retribution . . . . The occupational work of the vast majority of people is largely independent of their thought and speech. The professor's work *consists* of his thought and speech." And if a professor is fired for what he writes or says, then free speech and free expression in that society are gravely threatened.

That concept of academic freedom does not give a professor licence. He cannot stand up in a crowded theatre and shout "Fire" any more than anyone else. He has no right to try to indoctrinate students to a particular ideology or belief. He cannot preach Marxism, for example, without telling his classes that there might be two sides to certain questions; he cannot attempt to recruit students to join him in his beliefs in Scientology; and he cannot tell his students that the Arabs (or the Israelis) are all wrong. Some academics violate these rules and use their podium as a pulpit to preach a particular dogma to the susceptible young minds in their classes. These people are violating academic freedom and should be punished. But most academics understand that free speech has limits and that academic freedom is not boundless.

But if the academics understood, the politicians and university administrators have not always been clear on the question. And that is why tenure came to Canada. In the early 1940s, for example, Professor Frank Underhill, a distinguished Canadian historian at the University of Toronto, was threatened with dismissal because he had aroused the suspicions of Ontario politicians and the university administration. Underhill's loyalty was in doubt. It was wartime, but Underhill had not called for a Nazi victory nor had he spied. Underhill's crime was that he had said at a meeting that Canada was becoming an American nation and that the war had weakened Canadian ties to Britain. The collapse of France and a possible invasion of Britain, Underhill had said, meant that Canadians could "no longer put all our eggs in the British basket." Treason!

Underhill's 1940 truisms almost got him sacked by his university. The Leader of the Opposition in the Ontario legislature, the Premier of Ontario, senior members of the Board of Governors, and the press all bayed for his head. In the end, sense prevailed, but only after Underhill's friends mobilized and saved the great gadfly to fight again (but more quietly next time, please).

How could such a benign statement, even in wartime, have produced such a response? First, Canada was different then, more British in orientation, more closed-in and intolerant in its attitudes. Free speech was one of the reasons we were fighting the war; but who wanted free speech for agitators? In addition, the attitude of provincial politicians and university administrators was that professors had no right to, and indeed should be prevented from a public political position. Partisanship was for private citizens, journalists, or politicians, not for professors. After all, a member of the Board of Governors at the University of Toronto had said, "your university professor is in the same position as the school teacher. Is he not? Doesn't his salary come out of the taxes? People paying the taxes send their children to schools and they don't want politics preached to them . . . ."

That kind of attitude represented the worst possible case. On the whole, university administrations were prepared to defend the right of a professor to teach as he saw fit in the classroom. But, as Underhill's case showed, there was little or no inclination to protect the right of an academic to speak or write outside the university's hallowed precincts. There, he was on his own, and if his views flew in the face of the majority's beliefs, then it was the troublemaker's own lookout.

In such circumstances, most faculty members automatically exercised a degree of self-censorship on what they wrote and said. But in 1958, another great academic freedom case erupted in Canada. This was "the Crowe case" at United College in Winnipeg (now the University of Winnipeg). Harry Crowe was a history professor at United, a social democrat who had helped to create a faculty association at the small Manitoba school and who, as a result, had come into conflict with United's president. In 1957-58, Crowe was on leave from the college and teaching at Queen's University in Kingston, and a letter he wrote to a colleague back in Winnipeg, a letter that attacked policies of the United College Board of Governors, somehow found its way into the president's hands.

The case began out of those simple beginnings and

escalated into an affair that almost tore little United College apart, that drew national attention, that led to the firing of Crowe and the resignation of others who supported him, and that led inexorably to the establishment of tenure in Canadian universities. Harry Crowe had been discharged because of comments he made in a private and personal letter; he had been sacked by a Board of Governors that failed to confront him with any charges and that gave him no hearing. Compromises were sought repeatedly, but in the end they fell apart.

At this point, the Canadian Association of University Teachers was a new, small, and weak body. But the Crowe case was such a threat to everyone, such an assault on freedom of speech, that the Association was galvanized into action. A national office was opened and a senior academic hired to be the executive secretary. The CAUT created procedures and committees to defend academic freedom, an obvious necessity because few universities in the country had yet given any safeguards to their faculty. And the CAUT drafted guidelines that stated principles of academic freedom and tenure. The basic document said that "academic staff should have continuous (permanent) tenure after the expiration of a short, specified probationary period. Appointments should be terminated only for adequate, specified cause, and only by means of fair procedures." In other words, the national association of Canadian professors had come out for tenure as the best way to protect academic freedom; the emphasis on fair procedures also suggested that the CAUT wanted "the principles of natural justice" to be those on which tenure cases should be based. After the Underhill and Crowe cases, who could disagree with that?

Some did, most notably university administrations that could see their power to hire and fire at will being constrained. But over the next decade, circumstances altered dramatically in Canadian higher education. There was a vast expansion as university education suddenly became popular, patriotic, and necessary. A faculty member with a completed Ph.D. became a scarce commodity on the job market, and the universities that lagged behind in pay or perquisites could not get the staff they needed. Nor could they get faculty if they did not offer tenure. By the beginning of the 1970s, almost every Canadian university held out the promise of tenure to its staff, although the procedures by which it was awarded were not always those sought by the CAUT; over time, however, the procedures were brought into line. Tenure was in place and academic freedom was secure.

So, also, were the jobs of the faculty. Somehow in the course of the 1960s and 1970s, tenure transformed itself from a device to protect academic freedom into a system of defensive entrenchments designed to resist each and every assault on the job security of the faculty. Now the CAUT cannot argue that no one should ever be dismissed. The Association's "Primer on Tenure" says that "a tenured professor can be dismissed for cause – such as gross misconduct, incompetence or persistent neglect." In effect, the CAUT agrees that a professor can be fired if found *in flagrante delicto* with the president's spouse at high noon in front of the campus cafeteria. Other causes, by their very nature, are almost unprovable.

Is that too strong a claim? The 1983 president of the Canadian Association of University Teachers, Dr. Sarah Shorten, recently wrote that academics faced a major task. "We must explain to the public that procedures exist in all our institutions for the termination of those proven not to be fulfilling their responsibilities, and that termination in the event of fiscal exigency is not in conflict with the principle of tenure."[1] She is correct – there is a job of explaining to do. But while procedures to fire the incompetent do exist, how often have they been used? How many cases are there of tenure being removed from faculty members in Canadian universities in the last decade and a half?

One professor at the University of British Columbia observed that "wherever three professors are gathered together, one can hear stories of tenured academics who have used their tenure as a licence for terminal laziness, but," he said, "very few of them get away with it for long. The machinery exists to fire them if necessary." The machinery exists but it has become rusted with disuse. The best data, that from the CAUT itself, suggests that twenty-five academics have lost tenure in the last fifteen years.[2] There are now 33,000 academics employed in Canada's universities. Are there only twenty-five incompetents who have taught in the university system? Were they the only ones persistently to neglect their students and their duties? The law of averages is still in force, we think, and to ask the question is to answer it.

Whose fault is it if the universities have not been weeded more vigorously? The CAUT notes that it is the duty of university administrations to take action. "If administrators cannot bring themselves to face the unpleasantness of an arbitration [on dismissal]," the CAUT says, "the fault lies with the administrators, not with the faculty." Ultimately that is correct, and university administrations have been extremely lax in cleaning house. But the CAUT position is a shameful evasion of responsibility, an appalling passing of the buck. If the administration doesn't know of a case, how can it act? The incompetent's colleagues will know what is going on, the department chairperson will know if classes are not met or papers not marked; but university presidents can only learn of such things if someone tells them.

Whose fault is it? In the final analysis it is the faculty's responsibility. Academics always put great stress on their role in and responsibility for the governance of their universities, and there is no one so outraged as a professor whose rights have been infringed. But professors have been loath to move against their colleagues who fail to pull their weight. It is always easier to shunt poor old George off to teach in the night school or to schedule his classes for three p.m. on Fridays when no one ever attends classes than to begin the long and arduous procedure that is necessary to sack him for incompetence. In a sense, that is understandable. Few of us want to have our colleague's blood on our hands, and if the administration won't clear out the rot, why should we? What does it matter?

The Effects of Tenure

It matters. John Kenneth Galbraith, the distinguished Canadian-born American economist, was not joking when he said that "terminal laziness" is "a much cherished aspect of academic freedom." To the public and to those in the universities who have not fallen victim to the prevailing lassitude, tenure has become a form of protection for the featherbedders and the incompetent. Just once get tenure and never again, *never again*, will a professor have to face a review of his work that might threaten his job. Most academics get tenure in their late twenties or early thirties – and for the next thirty-five years they are safe. They might not be promoted to full professor or, the ultimate accolade, university professor; they might not be named a Fellow of the Royal Society of Canada; they might not win some of the major academic prizes; they may not receive as high a salary as those who work hard and publish; but they will not be sacked. They are as safe as anyone can be in the nuclear age – unless their university goes bankrupt.

Again, so what? Universities religiously claim to be in search of academic excellence. That is their reason for existence, their only purpose. They exist to train students to think, to read critically, to write with precision. They teach generations of students how to think about the world and how to tackle the problems of the present and the future in a humane and rational way. To instruct in a university is a challenge, and only the highly skilled should do it. University instructors are also paid to press back the frontiers of knowledge. To do research in history, for example, involves endless hours poring over the detritus of the past in archives; it involves trying to assemble the data on long-dead civilizations or on last decade's general election; and it involves the hard-slogging work of attempting to put that information into print in a form that will hold a reader's attention and possibly even affect the way he perceives his world. That, too, is an important task.

To help its faculty do its work, the university gives its members certain important concessions. The normal Canadian teaching load is three courses, each nominally of three hours a week. Those classes might have two students or 400; they might involve endless hours of marking and correcting and meeting with students, or they might involve almost none. Classes run only from September to mid-April with good holidays at Christmas and a reading week in one, or sometimes both, of the two terms. Administrative work can ordinarily be evaded by those determined to do so. Some faculty go out to the campus twice a week during teaching time; others might go three or four times. If the professor's job is conscientiously tackled, his teaching, administration, and research can run eighty hours a week; if leisure is the goal, the job can be done in ten hours. The system is easy to rip off, and too many take advantage of it.

Those that do are essentially unassailable. If a faculty member with tenure meets his classes, marks his papers, and holds an occasional office hour, he is safe. No one will object too strenuously if he fails to do his share of committee work. No one will complain if he fails to publish anything year after year. "I'm working on a big project," he might say if pressed. "I don't know when it will be ready. And I might not even publish it when it is ready." The students, dazzled by their professor's verbal skills, say nothing; the faculty members are certain to be dubious, but there are, after all, many cases where long processes of germination did produce splendid flowers of scholarship. And, of course, George is a good fellow, isn't he? George's neighbours may wonder how it is that he can go to Florida every December and to Europe each and every summer, but then they assume that is what every professor does.

Then there are sabbaticals. Almost every Canadian university gives each professor one year in seven to use for research. Ordinarily from 75 to 100 per cent of salary is paid during a sabbatical year, and each professor is entitled to a sabbatical as a right. Unionized universities have sabbaticals written into their contracts; at the others, it is a hallowed and sacrosanct part of the professoriate's terms and conditions of employment.

Sabbaticals are vital to the hard-working researchers on campus. They provide the chance to tackle a major research project without the distractions posed by students, by marking exams, and by committee meetings. They give a professor a chance to write a book, to hammer the typewriter (or word processor) day after day and to see a manuscript grow into something important. Sabbaticals are crucial to scholarship.

But sabbaticals have been shamefully abused under the protection afforded by tenure. At most Canadian universities, there is no requirement that a professor returning from sabbatical report in detail on what he has accomplished. No one asks if he sat on a beach in the south of France or if he stayed in his attic and worked. No one keeps a record of what was accomplished; no one examines the performance on the last sabbatical when it is time to grant the next one. Nor does anyone take a look at the faculty member's record during the intervening six years to ensure that research has been underway or that conscientious teaching has been performed. In other words, just as tenure has been perverted into job security, so, too, have sabbaticals been distorted by the effects of tenure into well-paid holidays – at public expense – with no hard requirement that the individual or the university have anything to show for it.

It's a good life for George, our mythical but all too real professor. He can sleep late most mornings, read the newspaper, or tinker with his stereo. He can perform the minimum requirements of his job and still count on safety in it. And every seventh year he gets sixteen months off work – the summer, the academic year, and the next summer – on sabbatical. A good life indeed.

The reader might wonder how George ever received tenure in the first place. A. E. Malloch of McGill University recently wrote about the group dynamics that often affect such decisions. It is, after all, peer evaluation that determined George's fate, and the dynamics of a group are always subtle. "A peer group is capable of closing ranks to protect one of its weaker members . . . . It is reassuring when members of a department stand up for a colleague who is doing worthwhile work, but who had little talent for self-presentation." But sometimes mistakes are made, as George demonstrates so well. "Consider the peers," Malloch writes, "who, out of a sense of professional solidarity, persuade themselves that a colleague, amiable and not obviously incompetent, deserves to be granted tenure. No harm done? That remains to be determined by several generations of students."[3]

If there was a shortage of qualified people to fill George's place, this might be less important than it is. In the late 1960s, back when George was considered a promising young scholar, the tendencies that even then were apparent could be overlooked in the face of the need to staff Sociology 201 or Psychology 202 or History 203 with their hordes of students. But today? Today, there are substantial numbers of Ph.D.s without university jobs. Some are actually driving taxis; more move on an endless hegira from one-year appointment to one-year appointment, dragging their families and their hopes across the country. Some of these displaced scholars are very good indeed, hard-working, active publishers with an interest in their students. What is to become of them?

Some, safely in the university system, argue sagely that these new Ph.D.s should seek out alternate employment. The civil service or business perhaps. But the public service does not hire any longer, and in the 1980s business is trying to survive, not to take a chance on hiring a Ph.D. in economics that no one at head office can understand. Can anyone seriously believe that is a credible alternative?

Leo Groarke, a graduate student in philosophy, wrote in the *CAUT Bulletin* that it would be more reasonable to say that "all qualified individuals should compete for positions, and those who are less qualified – whoever they may be – should look for some alternative." The tenured will not like that suggestion. But the young philosopher suggests that the only grounds they could have for rejecting his argument is the "unwarranted assumption that academics who already have positions have some inalienable right to keep them (despite the consequences for others)." Groarke's argument is hard to fault. So is his point that while tenure has protected academic freedom and is important for that reason, "it is equally important to take away the shield that tenure has provided for those who could not compete in conditions of free and equal competition." That, too, is difficult to counter. "In recent times," Groarke charged,

> the injustice of the tenure system has never been so blatant as it is today. With the scarcity of academic jobs and the over-abundance of Ph.D.s, the standards required of new academics have steadily escalated, and tenure is denying young academics the right to compete for jobs on the basis of equality. Any just society must allow its citizens equal access to job opportunities, and the academic job market can be no exception . . . .
>
> How can one honestly accept a system that parrots on about academic excellence, but refuses jobs to individuals who may be better qualified in teaching and research (not to mention future potential) than many of those within the comfortable pews? There is no justice in a system which makes individuals second-class citizens because they were born 10 or 20 years too late.[4]

Very simply, we believe that this case is unanswerable. If the universities are to give people like Groarke a chance, if they are to do their job effectively, then tenure must go.

An End to Tenure

There are right and wrong ways to eliminate tenure. Sometimes provincial governments seem to want to hit out at tenure as a way of striking at faculty that, they think, oppose the government en bloc. In British Columbia, for instance, the Social Credit government in 1983 moved with great vigour to ram a program of reorganization through the legislature. Civil servants, the aged, the infirm – these were the people to be victimized, and among those to feel the province's lash were universities and their faculty. British Columbia had already reduced its support per student significantly – down 24 per cent in real terms since 1972 – and the province ranked ninth out of ten provinces in university operating grants. Now, in the interests of "restraint," the government proposed to eliminate job security for public-sector employees, a group that included the professoriate. In other words, Bill 3, the Public Sector Restraint Act, gave university administrations the power to impose layoffs unilaterally. Tenure in British Columbia was gone.

The University of British Columbia Faculty Association challenged the Universities Minister (himself a tenured professor at UBC) to include explicit protections for academic freedom and university autonomy in the Bill, but the Minister refused. As a result, as UBC's president pointed out, "If the freedom to speak on consequential matters is imperilled, or if impediments to academic freedom exist, provincial universities will be unable to attract or retain leading scholars in any area of study . . . . B.C. could well become an academic backwater . . . ." So it could. And even though the provincial government did concede that faculty already on staff would not be affected by Bill 3 and that only newly hired faculty would not be eligible for tenure, the net result has been massive uncertainty in the face of something that smacks of political repression. That is not the way to redress the inequities of tenure.

On the other hand, as Michael Walker of the Fraser

Institute, the *eminence grise* behind Social Credit's restraint program, pointed out, the government's actions had shed some light on a few of the darker corners of academe. To those who claimed that tenure was necessary to ensure academic freedom, Walker answered that "It may just as easily yield an enclave of single-minded individuals who, under the protections of tenure, are able to systematically ensure that views (both scientific and political) contrary to their own are not represented in their department or university." A rash charge offered by a right-wing economist? Perhaps, were it not for the fact that at one university in Ontario in recent years a social work professor was denied tenure because he was the sole non-Marxist in his department. It took lawyers and an arbitration procedure to secure justice for him. Walker then observed that universities have to be able to change their course offerings to keep up to date and to serve the needs of society. "As students increasingly enrol in the 'hard' disciplines like science and commerce, more classes in these fields ought to be offered and fewer classes in the 'soft' disciplines."

But, Walker goes on, "the dean's dilemma is that resources must continue to be devoted to these less popular disciplines because, in part, there are so many tenured teachers in those areas. Elimination of tenure would make possible a more realistic and productive allocation of existing educational budgets."[5]

There is a spurious logic to Walker's marketplace thinking. If students want to study commerce instead of philosophy, they should certainly be allowed to do so. But do we then eliminate philosophy – or history or English – from the university curriculum? Can a university be worthy of the name if it is just a trade school that prepares students to fight it out in the business jungle? Or is a university a place where philosophy must be taught, even if relatively few students choose to major in it? Indeed, one can argue, and one should argue, that no student should be permitted to graduate from a Canadian university in the 1980s without some understanding of ethics, without a knowledge of Canadian, American, or European history, and without the capacity to speak and write clearly. Surely those things are just as important as the mastery of the case study method bowdlerized from the Harvard Business School. Walker's denunciation of tenure is as wrongheaded as his economics and as foolish in intent as the government he so thoroughly influenced.

In Ontario, a different technique seems to be under contemplation. The Education Minister in December 1983 announced the formation of a committee to study a restructuring of the province's fifteen-university system. A few years earlier, another committee had looked at the Ontario universities and proposed that there should be one comprehensive university offering a full range of programs at all degree levels; that there should be four full-service universities with a more restricted range of programs; and that there should be four or five special-purpose institutions. In this plan, some universities were to be closed while others were to be juggled into undergraduate program institutes.

The new committee apparently has a fresh mandate, and it is bound only by the Minister's carefully hedged promise that no university will be shut down and her pledge that the government might consider special allocations for "faculty renewal and adjustments" necessary to carry out the committee's plans. The 1981 committee had pointed to the large sums involved in restructuring if such a plan entailed, as it surely must, the cost of compensation for fired faculty.

No one yet knows what plans the committee will present. Perhaps a plan for the rationalization of the Ontario system, a rationalization that most would agree is necessary, can be accomplished gradually and without wholesale slaughter. Perhaps. But the one certainty is that any plan that calls for drastic change will upset many applecarts and lead to protests. Faculty hired on the promise they could teach graduate students will not be pleased to find their university turned into a special-purpose institution, one little different from the community colleges.

It is a sad fact that Premier William Davis, the Education Minister who largely created the Ontario system in the 1960s, is now presiding over its demolition. If British Columbia is ninth in operating grants to its universities, Ontario is tenth, and its campuses have been squeezed so long and so hard that there is no longer any fat to slice away. Now a massive reorganization is hinted with one of its major intentions clearly being to shatter tenure and to permit a massive revamping of departments and programs.

The way to remove tenure, however, is not with a British Columbia blunderbuss or an Ontario restructuring. Both substitute a false economic rationality for common sense. If tenure must go, and we believe it must unless the profession exercises its responsibilities more toughly and honestly than it has, the way to proceed is to substitute a system of long-term contracts for job-security tenure. Such a process would save what must be saved; that is, the academic freedom aspect of tenure has to be protected, enhanced, and made inviolate. But if renewable five-year contracts were substituted for the appointments without term that characterize the present system (and that have become licences for sloth), then an element of flexibility would be injected into the system.

With renewable contracts, there would be a continuous incentive for faculty members to work, produce, and improve. There would be a chance for universities to make changes in staff where the faculty were notoriously weak. And there would be some opportunity – certainly more than there is at present – for good graduate students to look toward the prospect of a university post.

But there are problems in renewable contracts. In their quest to save money, it is not inconceivable that university administrators might try to sack the highly paid at the end of a contract, reasoning deviously that three junior faculty could be hired to replace one senior. This can be countered to some extent by obliging universities to search for an equivalent faculty member and only hire a replacement of a different status when that equivalent cannot be found.

And who will decide who is or is not performing? This cannot be done by administrators; instead, committees of peers must undertake this job, however distasteful it might be. If such committees are elected at large, then no good will emerge from the process. There are always more of the weak than the strong at every university. But if the faculty members must be senior scholars, respected by all, then the process might work.

There will be upset on a major scale with renewable contracts, and we recognize this. We would never suggest this kind of system if we did not feel that the existing system has failed. The CAUT has failed to stand up for quality, and its constituent faculty associations have been worse. We can understand the group solidarity that leads professors to close ranks against a cruel world; but the result has been the virtual ruination of our universities.

We know that our colleagues will not leap to their feet to cheer this proposal. At one Ontario university, a suggestion that appointments to teach in the graduate faculty should be of limited term and subject to assessment before reappointment met with cries of outrage. "Periodic review of an academic person who has already met standards constitutes a serious threat to academic freedom," a letter printed in the faculty association newsletter fumed. But why? Why should academics alone be able to benefit from the perquisites of their profession without being subject to review? Why should the next generation of professors and professionals be taught by those who may have failed to keep up with current research and those who may not have done research themselves? This is simply arrogance. It is, especially given the provincial governments' determination to squeeze weak programs out of the country's university systems, nothing less than wilful blindness.

The current system cannot last unaltered. The options are wholesale and drastic change of the kind shoved down the professoriate's throat in British Columbia and suggested in Ontario or change that recognizes the fiscal realities of the present and the weaknesses of the current system of tenure. If that is the choice, and we think it is, then we are for the less drastic changes. If tenure can be replaced by a more rational arrangement that, while preserving academic freedom, allows for the elimination of the slothful, then the universities might yet survive as bastions of free inquiry. If tenure stands, however, then those who live in the ivory tower will have only themselves to blame when the whole structure comes crashing down.

Notes

1 "Why Bill 3 Affects Us All," *CAUT Bulletin* (December, 1983).

2 Allan Evans in *ibid.* (September, 1983).

3 "Academic Freedom and the Canadian Professor," *ibid.* (February, 1983).

4 "Tenure as Injustice," *ibid.* (February, 1982).

5 Quoted in *ibid.* (December, 1983).

CHAPTER VI

The Perishing of Publishing

Scholarly publishing, as we argued in Chapter V, is a crucial part of a university professor's role. It is important in assessing the faculty member's abilities in tenure and promotion decisions, of course. But it is also a crucial part of the professor's role within the university and the scholarly community at large. In essence, research and writing are what differentiate the university professor from the high school or public school teacher and the community college instructor. The teachers' contracts speak of their duty to instruct their students as conscientiously as possible; the university professor's contract states that his duties are to be found in the areas of teaching, service to the university and community, and research and publication. The difference is profound, and it is deliberate.

At York University in Toronto, for example, a draft policy statement on the responsibilities of faculty members said this:

> faculty members shall devote a reasonable proportion of their time to original research and innovative or reflective scholarly or creative work consistent with their academic stream. They shall make the results of such work available to the scholarly and general public through publications, lectures, and other appropriate means . . . .

This is quite simple and straightforward. Faculty members *shall* do research and *shall* publish. The use of "shall" instead of "may" makes clear that this is a directive and an instruction. In other words, all members of the faculty are expected to do research, to write, and to publish. Again, that is what differentiates the university from the public schools.

We know that many faculty members do not do research or publish, and we have suggested earlier that this does not ordinarily hurt their job security in the university. No one can say with confidence what percentage of Canadian academics are active publishing scholars for no one has ever conducted a comprehensive and rigorous survey of the Canadian academy. But there is one American survey, that taken at the end of the 1960s and the beginning of the 1970s by Everett Carl Ladd, Jr., and Seymour Martin Lipset, a distinguished American sociologist. Ladd and Lipset surveyed more than 60,000 professors in more than 300 institutions in the United States, and their results were startling.

How many books have you published?, faculty were asked. Four per cent said five or more; 22 per cent said one or two; and 69 per cent said none. How many publications do you have in the last two years?, the academics were asked. Eleven per cent said five or more books and articles, but 53 per cent said they had published nothing at all in the last two years. How many articles have you published in scholarly journals all told?, the professors were queried. Ten per cent said more than twenty, and 20 per cent said one or two; but 43 per cent of university faculty at the time of the survey had never published even one article.[1]

This data is suggestive, but some qualifications have to be made. Ladd and Lipset were surveying the American university scene with its sharp divisions among high-quality institutions, public and private schools, four- and two-year schools, junior colleges and community colleges. The Canadian scene is not truly comparable. Their data were mainly collected at the end of the 1960s, at a time when many junior faculty were just beginning their careers after a great burst of hiring. Their scholarly production, as yet, had scarcely had a chance to begin.

But those qualifications aside, the Ladd and Lipset data is extraordinary. Almost 70 per cent of faculty had never published a book. More than 40 per cent had never published a single article. More than 50 per cent had not published a word in the last two years. What the data say, in fact, is that in a society supposedly dedicated to research and the advancement of knowledge, about half were failing to live up to their responsibilities.

Is that situation any different today in the United States, or, more to the point, in Canada? Again, there are no comprehensive data, but our own observations suggest that the differences are minimal. In the authors' universities, there is almost no pressure and no incentive to publish, and many faculty simply do not do so. Many have *curriculum vitae* – or résumés – that stretch for dozens of pages, listing every committee on which they have served, every course they have taught, and tracing their graduate and undergraduate educations in painstaking detail; but there are no publications at all in many cases, and only faint indications of research in earlier stages of long-lasting university careers.

So what? Does this matter? As we suggested before, it does. Research is what keeps the teacher enthusiastic and up-to-date; it gives ideas and suggestions for future research that students can be encouraged to follow; and it is, very simply, part of a professor's duties.

Indeed, we consider it to be the main part of those duties. And research without publication is not sufficient. It is untested and untried, for the purpose of publishing one's research results is to test one's conclusions and ideas against the judgement of one's peers. Any professor can talk a good game and can readily dazzle impressionable undergraduates with his verbal fluency. Most professors have read more in the past and read more now than their students and there is, therefore, a too-easy acceptance of the idea that all must be on the cutting edge of knowledge. But unless that professor's ideas are tested in the academic marketplace, unless they are put out in a form that allows critics time to contemplate and probe them carefully, then they are just talk.

Scholarly articles and books are the usual form in which academics present their research results. Those publications are assessed and reviewed by experts who can praise or condemn the methodology and the data base and the style. To an academic, the praise of his peers is confirmation of his ideas and approach, and that is far more satisfying than the applause of students. In many fields, the praise of reviewers is also the way to win a chance to affect or even shape public policy. An economist, for example, who can derive new ways of measuring growth or unemployment might just find the federal government interested in his methods; a sociologist with expertise in studying alcoholism might just find the Addiction Research Foundation at his door. And – there is no point in avoiding this implication – such success in research can often win the professor major research grants or lavish contracts from government, foundations, or public agencies. To publish widely and well, to do research in germane subjects with skill, is to open many doors to academic success.

In other words, we believe in "Publish or Perish." Those simple words have become malign in recent years, a commentary on the system in force at the best American universities. There, a junior faculty member was hired as a lecturer or assistant professor and told that he had to have a book in three years. If not, he was out, farmed out to the boondocks at Podunk State Teachers College. If he passed that first hurdle, he was likely given tenure and told that if he expected promotion, he had to keep on producing. That was a tough system, and like all systems it had abuses. But it worked; it favoured the best and the brightest and the hardest working; and it ensured that the Harvards, Yales, and Princetons stayed high-quality institutions.

Publish or Perish never took root in Canada. In the late 1960s, our universities were stocked with hundreds of Americans seeking jobs in the booming provincial systems; many were casualties of the Publish or Perish system and they did not want to see their experiences south of the border replicated here. Other Canadian professors came from different traditions and shunned it as well, and Canadians, used to believing themselves second-rate, shied away from any system that promised excellence only at the price of shattered careers.

That was humane. But was it sensible? We think not and, as we look around the university now, we think it was disastrous. Safe in a system where Publish or Perish did not apply, many faculty simply atrophied. Their research dwindled into nothing, their attempts at writing became more and more infrequent. Why bother if no one cared? And no one did care.

This has gone on long enough and it is time to call a halt. Scholarship and publication are part and parcel of the responsibilities of every academic. Those who cannot perform are failing in their duties and should perish. Those who do publish and who do research should be brought forward and advanced. Publish or Perish, we believe, is essential if our universities are to become excellent.

The Long Arm of Government

Traditionally, research in Canada has been a private matter, a lonely effort by an individual professor trying to master a complex and complicated subject matter. There was the prospect of research grants; there was a possibility of getting a research assistant to do some of the hackwork; and there was the absolute certainty of devoting years to collecting the data and writing them up. The subject of the research was essentially a private matter between the researcher and his conscience. The university administration did not interject itself into this process; the academic's colleagues, while sometimes interested in the subject area, would not say nay; and the government, although it was usually the provider of funds to the granting agency, kept more than an arm's length away from the whole process.

This has recently begun to change in Canada. At most universities now the president or the director of research has to certify that a grant-seeking academic has the support of his institution. Those working on projects involving "human subjects" have to accept a series of requirements imposed by university ethics committees and attempt to ensure that electric shocks, for example, are not administered to the unwilling or the infirm. Such regulations make sense in some disciplines; in others they amount only to an interference with research. (The three authors of this book, to cite another example, regularly interview politicians. Our grant requests have to pass ethics committees when, in our view, we need protection more than the politicos we see.)

But it is the government role that has changed most significantly. In 1957 when the Canada Council was created, one of its mandates was to support scholarly research. At that time, the Council was independent, and the arm's length distance between recipients of Canada Council research grants and the government was genuinely respected. The Council received its moneys from the public purse, originally in the form of an endowment but after the mid-1960s in the form of annual grants. But it was genuinely independent: it could set up its own procedures, award grants in areas it selected and to those individuals it chose, and decide in which directions to throw its substantial weight. By the end of the 1960s, the government as provider of the cash was starting to seek more control over the process. If it was paying, the argument went, surely it had both the right and the responsibility to ensure that the country received some value for the public's money. The Social Science and Humanities Research Council of Canada was created, responsible to a minister of the crown, and the SSHRCC took over from the Canada Council the responsibility for supporting research in the humanities and social sciences.

Very quickly the government began to interject itself into the hitherto private world of the scholar. A series of research fields – the study of the aged or the North, for example – became designated as "strategic areas," and those who earlier had worked in such areas or who now were willing to switch their focus became virtually assured of funding without stint. Canadian Studies, a subject that we are treating in depth in Chapter VII, became a hot subject, and the government's support quickly led to the founding of new journals and academic associations and a vast network of scholarly conferences at home and abroad. And, to seem truly modern, the government set out to encourage collective research or research by a substantial number of scholars working as a team rather than the old-fashioned single scholar. The changes were substantial, and what they amounted to, or so many feared, was government interference with research.

Now, no one can argue that this interference has not thus far been relatively benign. Of course, the bureaucracy has grown; naturally, friends of the minister got posts in it; and, for sure, supporters of the government proposing expensive conferences and seeking assistance could usually count on a sympathetic ear in the Secretary of State's office. But that was relatively minor stuff. No one suggested that the peer appraisal that decided who should or should not get a grant had been politically influenced. At least, not yet.

But that is the concern. If the government is to put up the money, and if the money has to be accounted for as in any government department, then the apparatus of the state is well and truly involved. And if the state decides that some areas are more "strategic" than others, and if it suggests that group research is somehow more acceptable than individual research, then we are a long way along a road that will eventually see the government saying that Professor X is working on unimportant subjects and should not be supported, while Professor Y and his group of scholars are doing valuable research and deserve assistance. That is bad enough. The next step might well be that someone in government will say that X is a pinko or a Liberal while Y is a good Tory and hence should get his grant. That prospect frightens everyone.

Academics need government funds for their research, there can be no doubt of that. After all, in Canada, virtually all research in industry is also funded by government either in direct grants or in the form of tax write-offs. There is no argument against that, at least not from us, for we recognize that Canada is a small country where government intervention is necessary to help development.

But we do worry about the implications of the course the government is setting out on now. Big Brother is alive and well in Ottawa, poking his television lens and sensor into every corner, encouraging research here and turning a blind eye there. If the judgements were made only on grounds of quality, we could not complain. But government funding decisions seem to be based more and more on what Ottawa thinks best for us all. There is an element of social engineering here that is unhealthy, and academics as a rule have little confidence in the bureaucrats who operate the federal system. How can we? Too many of them were our students.

There is another side to all this, of course. Dr. William Taylor is the current president of the Social Science and Humanities Research Council of Canada and an able man. In a recent address, Taylor argued that the strategic grants program had not led to cuts in research support in other areas. On the contrary, he said, the money that went to the strategic areas helped protect independent research from budget cuts and eased the pressure on other budget areas. That may well be true – for now. Less reassuring was Taylor's question: Does a national government not have the duty to ensure that expenditures in research are well made and does it not have the duty to ensure that research should be facilitated on national problems? In other words, SSHRCC's president was arguing that while researchers have their freedoms and rights, so, too, do they have responsibilities and duties. Nor did the president see much to fear from the political motivation behind the strategic grants programs. That was "more than a little strong," he said, as "I don't think the Liberals would lose one seat over the strategics or gain one. I don't think this government or any other government would lose a single seat if it cut the Council budget in half and I don't think this government or any other would gain a single seat if it doubled the budget." Perhaps that was so, and perhaps Taylor was correct when he said that the academic attack on the strategic grants program sent a message to government that "as a professoriate of scholars, we sounded selfish, short-sighted and uninformed."[2]

Perhaps. But the road to state control of research has to begin somewhere, and many feared that the "strategics" were a big step along the way to that end. It is a long way from that program to the burning of books, but many were afraid for the future. And while it is too much to expect that the government's appointee to the top SSHRCC post should see things the way his clientele do, nonetheless one might have expected more sensitivity to academics' concerns.

The reader might well ask if this financial squabbling matters very much. Isn't this really about queuing up for money at the public trough? To some extent that is so, but genuine issues of importance are also at stake here. This is still a small country with a very small research community. Without government funding, researchers might flee to the south and research might dry up. In some areas, the government has the right (and, indeed, the duty) to organize and direct research – national defence-related subjects are just one such example. But what is new in the current dispute is that the government has interfered in areas that historically it considered unimportant. Who cares if a few academics do research into Shakespeare's plays or into party politics in England in the 1890s or into the

117

behaviour of crowds in the French Revolution? Academic research had always been a sideshow, valuable in and of itself primarily to those doing it and to that tiny community that read the books produced by scholars. Somehow that has begun to change in Canada. Some areas of research in the humanities and social sciences are now being given an importance above the others, and the state, implicitly if not yet explicitly, has said more money will be available for those areas. Does this distort the priorities of researchers in the academy? You bet it does. For example, if a researcher was intending to study the decade between 1957 and 1967 when Pearson and Diefenbaker jousted for supremacy, he might have trouble getting a grant for a straightforward appraisal of the times. But if he applied for a strategic grant under some such title as "The Effects of Age on Prime Ministerial Leadership in a Northern Climate: The Cases of John Diefenbaker and L. B. Pearson," his success would be assured. For some reason that frightens us; it should frighten others, too.

The End of Scholarly Publishing?

There is another way in which research and scholarly publication are threatened. What if there are no publishers willing to print scholarly books? What if there are no journals to publish research-based materials? What then?

On one level, to even raise the possibility of the end of scholarly publication seems alarmist. At the present time, the Social Science and Humanities Research Council funds 115 scholarly journals ranging from *Thalis: Studies in Literary Humour* to *Atlantis: A Women's Studies Journal* and from *Canadian Children's Literature* to the *Canadian Journal of Irish Studies*. Grants are for up to $27,000 a year. In addition, the

Canadian Federation for the Humanities and the Social Science Federation of Canada receive almost $1.25 million a year for grants in aid of the publication of scholarly books. These grants can go up to $7,500 to assist publishers to bring out academic books, and an average of 136 books a year (since 1973) have been so subsidized. How, then, can there be a crisis?

The problem is money. The director of the University of British Columbia Press said in 1981 that his problems sprang from the small print runs that most academic books require. If the run was 5,000 copies, a far larger run than that for most scholarly books, it would cost $4.10 a copy to print a 296-page book. Such a cost, of course, would not include overhead, distribution, advertising, or author's royalties, and it also excluded the bookseller's mark-up. On a run of 1,000, a figure that approximates the sales of most scholarly titles, the printing cost for the same size book would be $10.47 a copy. And on a run of 500, the expected sale for a very specialized title, the unit printing cost would be $18.27. When all the other costs are built in, that $18.27 cost balloons the price of the book to $40, and at that price the sales will almost certainly be less than the 500 copies expected.[3]

Those figures are from a scholarly publisher, a university press. Most of the university presses in English Canada – only UBC, McGill-Queen's, and the University of Toronto Press are substantial – can count on some support from their institutions, but those universities are already under pressure and cannot lend assistance much longer. It was just such a squeeze that almost forced the collapse of McGill-Queen's a few years ago. For commercial publishers the situation is as bad or worse. Ten years ago, companies such as Oxford, Macmillan, Clarke Irwin, and McClelland and Stewart actively published scholarly works, and smaller companies did so as well. Not any longer. Clarke Irwin has folded; Oxford University Press, despite its name, publishes no more than one academic book each year, and because Oxford is owned in England it is ineligible for a variety of grants that might let it do more; Macmillan now publishes only popular titles; and McClelland and Stewart, itself frequently in fiscal troubles, has cut back drastically in this area.

Part of the problem is, as we have suggested, the small size of the market. A large sale for a trade book in Canada is 10,000 copies, and only a very few books – the best of Pierre Berton or Peter Newman or Farley Mowat – ever sell as many as 50,000 copies. Those are substantial sales figures, of course, but the book industry is subject to all the problems of distribution that can beset a large and thinly populated nation. In addition, publishing almost alone among industries allows retail outlets to return unsold merchandise for full credit. This means that a title that does badly in the bookstores can come bouncing back to the publisher's warehouse three or six months after publication.

Even the once substantial library market is collapsing. University libraries in the palmy days of the late 1960s used to place standing orders for everything published, but that practice has long ago disappeared. So has the university habit of ordering multiple copies of important books so students seeking the book in the stacks could have a chance of finding it. Now only one copy of an important book will be purchased, and if staff cuts permit, it might be on the shelf in six months. The big city public libraries, facing high labour costs and increasing shortages of space, have also cut back. The result is that a once-sure market has dwindled away. There is no prospect that the situation will improve.

The scholarly publisher has the same problems, and he lacks even the possibility that some of his titles will catch the public's fancy and sell, sell, sell. This simply does not happen to arcane studies of Beowulf or detailed analyses of land tenure problems in Prince Edward Island. The result is an impossible situation.

If the university presses go under, and they are all in difficulties, it is a distinct possibility that there will be no outlet at all for the publication of scholarly books. Even if they do survive, it is extremely unlikely that a book buyer outside of Toronto, Montreal, or Vancouver will ever find a book by an academic author in a trade bookstore. The university presses have weak distribution systems, for one thing. They ordinarily permit booksellers only a 20 per cent mark-up, for another, instead of the 40 per cent allowed by trade publishers, and the bookstores as a result are reluctant to give the university presses scarce shelf space. And finally, everyone knows that no one reads scholarly books. Why then should a bookstore carry them? There is an element of self-fulfilling prophecy built into that.

In their efforts to hang on, some university presses, and some commercial publishers, too, are beginning to talk about eliminating academic author's royalties. The usual rate is 10 per cent, sometimes of the list price and sometimes of the net price (which is the list price less the bookseller's profit). If a book sells at $20, an author can expect a royalty of $2 per copy sold in the best circumstances. For an ordinary scholarly book, one that will sell, say, 1,500 copies over three years, the total royalty will be $3,000. That is not a bad sum, about enough to pay for a ten-day vacation in the sun at today's prices. But as a reward for five years' slogging it is small potatoes indeed. If the publishers carry on with their intention to cut out even this type of modest reward, there will be absolutely no financial reason whatsoever to write.

That will not stop those who do their research and

writing simply for love, but it will be yet another disincentive to those who do not want to work very hard. There are already enough academics in that category. An end to royalties might also encourage scholars to spend their time putting together collections of articles, writing texts, or turning their hands to pot-boilers in an effort to make money. Most university tenure committees tend to distinguish between serious work and pot-boilers, but trash, as always, pays more than serious work. It always has, and it always will. Do we really need any more of it?

Surely the situation is better in journal publication? It could hardly be worse, but once again the problem is money. At 1981 rates – to which at least 15 per cent must be added – it costs $40,000 to $50,000 a year to produce and distribute 1,500 copies of a quarterly journal of 400 pages a year. That is not a large journal. The *Canadian Historical Review*, for example, a journal with which the authors of this book have been closely associated, publishes more than 600 pages a year, has over 3,000 subscribers, and costs the University of Toronto Press, its owners, almost $80,000 a year.

Faced with such costs, journals are in trouble all across the country, desperately searching for better ways to reach their readers. The Social Sciences and Humanities Research Council thought it had found a better way a few years back when a commissioned report proposed that journals consider using modern technology to deliver their messages. For example, a journal with a small circulation might consider abandoning print entirely and distribute its issues on microfiche. The reaction to this suggestion was one of horror, and rightly so. It is difficult enough to read the contents of most scholarly journals even when the articles are printed on an ordinary page; if readers have to go to a microfiche reader and fiddle with dials – and contend with their fading eyesight and bifocals – no one ever again will read scholarly articles. The SSHRCC's report is in limbo for the moment, but in Ottawa old committee reports never die. The microfiche idea will be back.

With all these journals and with all those books receiving support, the reader might be forgiven for believing that there is no shortage, at least, of scholarly work being done. That might appear to be the case on superficial examination, but in fact there is a dearth. Earlier we suggested that the situation in Canada is likely much the same as in the United States where half the academic profession never writes a word. Our own experience as journal editors tends to sustain that impression as well. Very few journals in this country have comfortable high-quality backlogs. The *Canadian Historical Review*, for example, used to have up to two years' material on hand in the early 1970s when there were dozens of young professors researching and writing and seeking tenure and even more eager graduate students desperately trying to break into print. No longer. Now the young professors are middle-aged, paunchy, and tenured, and they have largely subsided into silence; and there are no longer as many graduate students as there once were. Too few jobs are available now or in the near future to encourage the best students to subject themselves to the rigours of a doctoral program without some assurance of a job at the end of the trail.

Nowadays, in consequence, a few articles make their way from journal to journal. Something rejected by the *Canadian Historical Review*, for example, may be sent to *Ontario History* or *Labour*; or it may go from one of these journals to the *Journal of Canadian Studies* or *B.C. Studies*. Sometimes it will be put back into the drawer for resurrection in a few years.

Our point is a simple one: surprisingly little new

research is underway. This shows in book publication, too. One of the authors of this book spent three years as a judge in the English-language non-fiction category of the Governor General's awards. What surprised him was how many books were published in his category each year – at least 400 in a dazzling array of picture books, tracts for the times, trade books, and cook books – and how very few scholarly books there were. At most, thirty-five ever found their way to the committee. Some truly technical studies were automatically eliminated, as were collections and edited works. But there were only a few titles each year.

There is a crisis in scholarly publishing then. On the one hand it is a crisis caused by high costs and by the understandable reluctance of commercial publishers and the growing inability of university presses to publish scholarly manuscripts. On the other hand, there is an almost perceptible drawing back by scholars from the whole convoluted process of research and writing. It is almost as if the entire academic community had become so demoralized that it has largely stopped performing its most important role. If that is so, it is a tragedy of major proportions.

Academic Gobbledegook

If the academics are giving up on scholarly research and writing, most readers in the general public have long since given up on academic books. Part of the problem is, as indicated above, the cost and poor distribution of academic books. But there is another reason. Scholarly communications are only rarely written in comprehensible English prose.

There are some shining examples of prose style among academic writers. Donald Creighton, for example, ranks as a stylist with any of the practitioners in our literature in his ability to convey mood. Here, for example, is a brief passage from Creighton's biography of Sir John A. Macdonald, a passage setting the scene for the Prime Minister's death:

It was the first of June. The Ottawa valley was bathed in heat and light. For two weeks there had been scarcely any rain. The sun rose blood-red at dawn and sank at night into a blood-red sky. Behind its drawn curtains, the great dim bed-chamber at Earnscliffe was drowsy with summer heat; and there he lay, wasted, silent, somnolent, but still alive. His splendid vitality, which he had used and abused so often and which had never failed him yet, was fighting a final, involuntary battle for his existence.

Creighton's prose moves and flows, sets the tone for the chapter that follows, and, unobtrusively, is soundly based on solid research. That is what good scholarly writing should be.

But the Creightonian model is now gone and forgotten. Instead we get social science English in place of prose. For example, a recent study of urban government included this passage:

Truncated systems, then, develop upward by being liberated from the confines of a predominantly exchange-based framework, but the more general media and resources are superimposed on, do not replace, the older, more specific ones. However superior diffuse support may be as a creator of system surpluses and new opportunities for development, all levels are necessary. The fused, top-heavy, traditionalist system, which outperforms the higher levels and ignores the lower ones, which tries to make general resources and media perform all system func-

125

tions, has as limited a performance capacity as the truncated system.

What can this mean? Can such language possibly convey any meaning at all to anyone but a committed specialist who simply has to read the book? Does it even convey meaning there?

This is not an isolated example, either in the book in question or in the scholarly literature generally. Consider this extract from a recent textbook on foreign policy:

The focus of such associative behaviour in the liberal-internationalist vision is a particular emphasis on practising the 'diplomacy of constraint'. This is designed to inhibit the unilateral exercise of preponderant American power in a manner unfavourable to Canadian and global interests. The primary instrument is the creation of a wide multilateral regime of common norms and the institutional machinery to make them effective. In overseas relations the exercise of constraint requires Canada to concentrate on those groups in which the United States is involved and to mobilize coalition partners in an effort to lessen American dominance. It further demands a continual effort to channel as much American behaviour as possible through multilateral institutions, where the restraining effects of institutional norms and informal persuasion can be applied most effectively.

What that is saying, we think, is that the Canadian relationship with the U.S. is a difficult one because the United States is so much more powerful. To deal with this, Canada prefers to treat with the Americans in international organizations where it can find like-minded friends and where the Americans cannot push as hard as they might in a one-to-one situation. Is there any reason why simple words of that sort could not have been used?

The reason why they are not employed is probably that academics feel unhappy if their fuzziness is immediately comprehensible to the reader. If a ten-dollar word is used, the reasoning seems to go, then the content must be high-powered; and if the bafflegab and buzzwords are employed, then even other academics will have to assume that the result is important. Only the general reader and the academic's poor students suffer from this silliness.

If the average reader has turned his back on scholarly publications, it is the academics, and their publishers who have allowed them to practise their gobbledegook, who are to blame. What is frightening is that simple prose is disappearing even in the areas where it has traditionally been a mark of good craftsmanship. History used to be comprehensible by all, but no longer. The influence of "cliometrics," the intrusion of a new social science history replete with the methodology and prose style of the social sciences, is fast turning history into a subject as unreadable and unpalatable as sociology or political science.

But, the reader says, won't Publish or Perish simply increase the amount of unreadable prose that is published? It might. But in a tighter scholarly publishing market, the university presses and the occasional commercial house that essays a scholarly book might feel emboldened to ask that the author write in simple English. That might help. The funding agencies that put up the money for scholarly journals might insist that a normal reader be able to understand articles. And the committees that assess promotion and tenure and that may some day, we trust, determine whether or not contracts should be renewed could also look at such simple matters as comprehensibility.

Of course, simple readability is not the only criterion of worth. Some published material is worthless, and some widely published scholars have little standing with their peers. We do not want to see a system where promotion is based only on the number of books or the number of pages published. Peer assessment is crucial. All we suggest is that good prose is as important in scholarly publishing as in every other kind.

Saving Graces

There are some simple remedies for these problems. But even simple remedies cost money, and there is not much chance that more money will be poured into academic grants and into publishing in the current climate. That is a pity, for without more aid scholarly publishing is likely to go the way of the dodo.

First, the publishers need more support. The university presses in particular have to receive an infusion of money to allow them to carry on. More money will let them pay their editors a living wage, and happy editors might actually encourage academic writers to write clearly and comprehensibly. More money might also let the university presses charge less for their books – and continue to pay royalties – and that must lead to larger sales and happier authors.

Unfortunately, the only place from which additional aid to the presses could come is from the government. And if the government is going to insist on greater control over publishing as a result, then that money would cost too much. This has been the net result of government financing of research; it should never become a product of government support for publishers. But if there are no other sources of money . . . ?

Within the university proper, there should be a greater effort to encourage research and writing. We have argued that no one is now hurt by a failure to publish. That must change. Those who do not publish should be punished, for example, by lifting their right to sabbaticals and by restricting severely their right to promotion. The universities should insist that their faculty live up to their responsibilities, and those who do not should be replaced.

But to publish, there must be university presses and scholarly journals. There are journals aplenty in Canada now, and there is a relatively substantial amount of money to subsidize scholarly publishing. But, as we have argued, the situation is precarious and the publishers have to be strengthened greatly. If this is done, then the universities will be in a position to clean house; if the publishers are left to wither and die, then the chance of strengthening the universities will be lost as well.

Notes

1 *The Divided Academy* (New York, 1975), pp. 152, 352-3.

2 M. Albagli, "An Innocent Lamb to the Slaughter?" *Social Sciences in Canada*, XI (September, 1983), p. 8.

3 Cited in *Quill & Quire* (December, 1981).

CHAPTER VII
Canadian and Other Useless Studies

At the end of the 1960s, Canadians suddenly discovered that they had an educational crisis on their
hands. The elementary and secondary schools were
teaching their children little about Canada, and what
they were teaching was rote learning about dated con-
stitutional acts, voyageurs in canoes, and a whole
series of stale clichés about French-English relations,
immigrants and labour, and the way the country worked.
No wonder the kids were fed up with Canadian history
and social science; no wonder "civics" was a bore; no
wonder Canadians still looked to Washington or, less
often now, to London or Paris as the metropolis and to
New York and Los Angeles as the taste centres of their
world.

And the universities? The universities, it turned out,
were teaching very little about Canada at all. The professors were instructing their students in sociology and
economics and political science, but only a few courses
in these and other subjects dealt with Canada, and in
some subject areas, particularly English literature,
there was scarcely a Canadian-centred course in the
entire country. Many subjects were taught from American textbooks designed for American students, and
there were dozens of courses in all disciplines where
Canada was at best an analogy and at worst an extra-
polation to which data from south of the border were

assumed to apply. Immigrants to the United States were, after all, just like immigrants to Canada, weren't they? And French Canadians were not very much different than blacks or Puerto Ricans in the U.S., right?

The American Academic Invasion

What had caused this extraordinary state of affairs? The easy answer was the Americans. In the middle and late 1960s, when the universities were ballooning at an amazing rate, thousands of American academics came to Canada to staff the new departments and swell the size of older ones. This made sense to everyone. The universities had to have the faculty to teach the hundreds of thousands of students who had suddenly decided that a B.A. or B.Sc. was absolutely necessary for their job prospects. The new universities, erected on scrub land outside the cities, were particularly desperate, and while they all tried to get the best people they could in a seller's market, all were only too grateful to take any who were willing to come to the frozen north. So long as the recruits had their "union card" in the form of a complete or almost complete Ph.D., they were welcome.

And the Americans came for a variety of reasons. Some were casualties of the tough standards applied at the first-rate U.S. universities, victims of Publish or Perish who had been assured that Canada was different. Some came because they were offered more money. Others, looking for a job, liked the idea of going somewhere foreign. Still others were fleeing the breakdown of American society that seemed so evident in the Vietnam War, in the plethora of political assassinations, and in the police riots that had so marked the Democratic convention of 1968 in Chicago. Canada was stable and safe, different but similar.

Inevitably, there were good and bad in this huge group of academics. Some were first-rank scholars who came, taught, and stayed; some were here for a two-year tax holiday, beneficiaries of a rip-off perpetuated by the tax systems of the two countries that let an American working here for two years pay taxes to neither government. Many of the newcomers adapted quickly to Canada; others never came to accept cities that did not sell the *New York Times* on every corner. But all the Americans came with their own cultural baggage, a sure feeling that American scholarship, American examples, and American methods were the best, ripe for export to backward Canada.

Probably they were partially correct. Some Canadian university departments in the 1960s were still bravely flying the Union Jack in spirit. There was tea at 4 p.m. and good chat about the old days at Magdalen College, Oxford. There was the annual voyage home each May, usually to a Cotswolds cottage and almost never to do research. The newcomers – and the Canadian academics hired in this period – were completely uninterested in that nonsense. They wanted to talk about Berkeley or Harvard, not Oxford. They brought new ideas for courses, for humanities and social sciences divisions, and for general education programs, and they also had strange ideas about how the academic universe in Canada could be re-ordered.

It took some years for the reaction to develop. The American academics were so evidently needed to educate the children of the baby boom. The plan, such as it was, was simple: the baby boomers, once educated, would take their place in the university stream and in due course take over the teaching jobs held by the Americans who would either move on or assimilate.

But there was one problem. The unprecedented growth of the 1960s was not a permanent condition, and the retrenchment fell upon the universities in the 1970s. There were no longer new jobs for Ph.D.s trained in Canada, and there were no longer jobs in the United States to which the Americans could return. Those here were here to stay, doomed to grow old together in Lethbridge, St. Catharines, or Wolfville.

The net result, particularly in the new universities, was that whole departments were American. At York University in Toronto, for example, early in the 1970s fifteen of sixteen departments in the Faculty of Arts and Sciences had American majorities. At most universities, much of the hiring had resulted in the appointment of Americans. Some departments, in fact, seemed to be recruited *en bloc* from one or two U.S. graduate schools, and some as a result simply refused to hire Canadians with a doctorate from another place, and particularly with one from a Canadian graduate school. There was a problem.

Nationalism in the Universities

Part of it was that the late 1960s was a period in which Canadian nationalism was on the rise. It was the Centennial, Expo '67, the coming of Pierre Trudeau – and it was Vietnam, Lyndon Johnson and Richard Nixon, and rioting in Washington and Detroit. Suddenly Canada looked pretty good to those of us fortunate enough to live here, and suddenly there was the shocking realization that none of the universities were teaching Canadian students about their country.

That claim was not entirely true, of course. Canadian history was a staple in each and every university, and there was almost always a wide variety of political science courses on Canada at the disposal of students. But in truth there really were no courses in Canadian literature or sociology, precious few in economics or geography, and only occasional courses in other disciplines. On one level, this was not quite as serious as it seemed. Students had to learn about other societies and cultures to be considered "educated" and to be able to understand their own country. The difficulty was that in some universities and some disciplines it was almost impossible to learn anything about Canada.

Once perceived, the problem was tackled head-on, happily without quotas on foreigners or the limitation of each and every administrative post to Canadian citizens. The number of courses offered in Canadian subjects quickly expanded across the country, and universities began to pay attention to the way they hired. Under the lash of the Department of Manpower and Immigration, they advertised in Canadian journals and newspapers, usually phrasing advertisements to read that "in accordance with Canadian immigration requirements, this advertisement is directed to Canadian citizens and permanent residents." In effect, foreigners could now be hired only if no suitably qualified Canadian was available. The result was that the only "aliens" hired by the late 1970s were those for which there was a demonstrable need. There were violations of this rule, of course, but in general the system worked.

Some were still unhappy. The Association of Universities and Colleges of Canada, the umbrella organization of university administrations, in late 1972 created the Commission on Canadian Studies and put it in the care of Thomas H. B. Symons, the founding president of Trent University in Peterborough, Ontario. The Symons Commission advertised widely for briefs as it sought to discover what was taught about Canada, who taught it, where it was taught, and the kinds of archival and library resources that could be used by teachers and students. The Commission – Symons was the only member and he often was given to referring to himself as "The Commission" – was also to examine the possibilities for encouraging Canadian Studies abroad.

Symons' report came out in 1975 (followed by a later volume in 1984 – Symons was not exactly speedy) and it painted a dreary picture. There were too few courses on Canada in the universities, it said, largely referring to a situation that was already being remedied, and what the country needed was a concentrated effort to get more Canadian Studies into the universities and a much greater effort abroad so that the British, French, Germans, Italians, and Japanese could learn about Canada's many accomplishments. Those were worthy goals, and there is no doubt that Symons' report, published as *To Know Ourselves*, made a substantial impact in the press and in Ottawa.

But some scholarly associations were worrying that an increased emphasis on Canada at a time of retrenchment might mean cutbacks in other areas. The Canadian Historical Association, for example, pointed out that "over one quarter of all historians in Canada are 'Canadianists' .... There are, however, many areas which are barely covered in Canadian universities." Latin America, Japan, China, Africa, and India were often barely taught, and that disturbed the historians. "There is little doubt that the report's strictures on the lack of attention to Canadian subjects in Canadian universities applied very well not long ago," the CHA said. "Now we may know ourselves. Can we yet know others?"[1]

What's Wrong with Canadian Studies?

Nonetheless, Canadian Studies was the inevitable result. And at this point the authors must explain themselves. All three of us teach Canadian history and write and research about Canada, so we can scarcely be seen as objecting to the study of Canada. And yet all three of us are opposed to Canadian Studies. How can this be?

The reason is simple. Canadian Studies has come to be almost a discipline in its own right. As one early proponent defined it, Canadian Studies "attempts to survey the Canadian experience as an integrated study and encompasses a number of the traditional disciplines – history, politics, economics, archaeology, sociology, geography, architecture, environmental studies, music, native studies, art and literature in English and French . . . if it has a rationale [Canadian Studies] must be more than isolated and compartmentalized studies in the traditional disciplines." Canadian Studies, he said, "must attempt to use probing interdisciplinary approaches to explain the Canadian experience as a whole . . . . Otherwise a shallow piecemeal effect can be created in the mind of the student."[2] That was the goal, and in pursuit of it there are now Canadian Studies journals, an Association of Canadian Studies, Canadian Studies programs with courses at the undergraduate and graduate levels, Canadian Studies conferences, and a vast array of prizes for work in Canadian Studies. In other words, the Symons Commission had made Canadian Studies A GOOD THING, and governments and universities hastened to jump on the bandwagon.

This was not a uniquely Canadian phenomenon. In the United States, for example, the rise of black consciousness led to the creation of Black Studies programs, and the rebirth of Indian militancy in both Canada and the U.S. produced Native Studies programs. The same thing happened with women's courses, with Hispanic-American courses, with ethnic history. Suddenly the old disciplines no longer seemed trendy enough to students and many professors, and certainly the old departments were unworthy of additional support by government. If a university wanted to get specially earmarked grants or if it wanted to appeal to private donors, it had to be at the cutting edge, and in Canada, in particular, that meant Canadian Studies.

Typically, a Canadian Studies program had a chairperson or a director in charge and one or two full-time professors on staff. But typically, too, most programs simply drew from the array of Canadian courses already offered in the traditional disciplines. An undergraduate might take one or two core courses in Canadian Studies, courses that threw together all the students with two or three faculty, but the rest of his program would be made up from courses in history, politics, economics, geography, or literature. In other words, beyond a few courses that were specifically designated as Canadian Studies, the principle was that of the smorgasbord.

What could possibly be wrong with that? What is wrong with it is that the students of Canadian Studies absolutely failed to get a solid disciplinary training. In Chapter IV, we bemoaned the excessive specialization that now characterizes the honours programs in most Canadian universities; that is not the problem here. The flaw in Canadian Studies is that the students take too little in any one discipline to learn anything concrete. A "shallow piecemeal effect" can be and is being created, along with unhealthy introspection and self-congratulatory navel-gazing. And paradoxically, the students in Canadian Studies take too few courses about other societies and cultures to be able truly to appreciate Canada.

Claude Bissell, the former president of the University of Toronto, said it all very well. "It is no service to the study of Canadian subject matter to detach it too abruptly from an established discipline. The Canadian historian must know European and American history; and the Canadian literary historian and critic cannot erect a structure on the basis of Canadian writing alone, which derives much of its strength and fascination from the adaptation of European models." Bissell goes on to argue that too early and too exclusive a concentration on Canadian literature, or history or geography, "is bad for the student – it induces flatulence in critical theory. I am sceptical of an undergraduate programme in 'Canadian Studies'," Bissell says, because such a program "is akin to other curricular developments that tie a whole range of disciplines to a particular aspect of a subject, e.g., 'women's studies', – it is difficult not to turn such programmes into didactic exercises, and to make the search for truth the search for the holy grail."[3] Precisely.

And what of the graduate level? James Page, a former community college teacher who worked with the Symons Commission and who eventually came to rest as the official in charge of Canadian Studies in the Department of the Secretary of State in Ottawa, was critical of Canadian universities. They were simply not doing their job, he said. "There are no programs in Canadian studies at the doctoral level anywhere in this country," Page noted in late 1981. "Ironically, students who want to do Ph.D. work in Canadian studies are forced to travel to the American universities that offer such programs."[4]

In one sense, that is unfortunate because there is probably a place for Canadian Studies at the graduate level. Bissell wrote that "The problem with all interdisciplinary studies" such as Canadian Studies "is that they become vital only in the mind of the individual who can fuse insights from a variety of sources."[5] And there are few such individuals. In other words, Canadian Studies as a discipline can work only with that rare bird who can think in an interdisciplinary mode, and such young people are only to be found in graduate schools. But to teach and train those few, departments or centres of Canadian Studies are unnecessary. Instead, it would be better to have that kind of advanced student work directly with a committee of like-minded faculty drawn from one or more departments. The doctoral degree could be given by one of those departments, and there would be no difficulty in ensuring that the specialty in Canadian Studies was clearly delineated. After all, a Canadian historian's doctorate is in history, and no one doubts that the historian is a specialist in Canada.

But there are other problems with Canadian Studies, too. James Page noted some of them when he pointed out that "Canadian studies experts still lack prestige in the academic community. Coordinators of Canadian studies programs are often junior faculty members who are underpaid, over-worked, and receive little recognition from tenure and hiring committees for the academic value of their efforts." The need now, Page argued, is for a study to determine, among other things, if "participation in a Canadian studies program advance[s] an academic career or does it destroy opportunities for academic advancement?"[6]

This is a delicate area, one that is somewhat painful to explore. One reviewer of *To Know Ourselves* pointed out that while Symons was "envious of the extent of American Studies programmes in the United States," he did not consider why such institutions as Harvard and Yale did not encourage area studies of any kind, nor that "American Studies is widely perceived in the United States to be unwieldy, amorphous and intellectually second-rate."[7] In other words, to over-generalize, in the U.S. the best academics have shied away from American Studies. In Canada, the same phenomenon has occurred with Canadian Studies.

In part, this is the usual resistance to something new and mildly unsettling. Like other people, academics crave the assurances provided by traditional structures and they are frightened by the new. A political scientist, naturally enough, prefers to stay in his own field. But say that scholar's career is blocked by poor teaching or a failure to publish, or even by the malevolence of his chairman? Canadian Studies might be a useful way to escape, a chance to make a fresh start in an area that is certain to be well-financed, to attract students, and to have governmental support.

We do not suggest for one moment that everyone in Canadian Studies is there because of career difficulties. But some are. And in any university today it is simply not possible to make a fresh start – one's reputation as a good scholar or a poor one, as a publisher or a non-publisher, goes along. Unless the very best specialists in Canada are in Canadian Studies – and they are not – then Canadian Studies, like American Studies in the U.S., will lack academic credibility. All the James Pages in the world can claim that professors are being held back only because of their Canadian Studies specialty, but that will be simply untrue.

The simple fact is that Canadian Studies has fallen into the hands of the academically weak. Again, that is an over-generalization that fails to take into account the good scholars who have worked and are working in this area. But it is a defensible generalization. Few of the major scholars in the country are involved with Canadian Studies; fewer still have any desire to be involved with it, in part at least because of those who are involved in the area and those who control the associations and the government funding.

The Canadian Studies Empire

We have seen signs of this problem overseas, of all places. The Canadian Studies empire, as designed by Symons and External Affairs in Ottawa. stretches to the United States, Britain, Germany, Italy, Japan and, most recently, to India these days, and there are endless series of national and international conferences each year to which the Canadian Studies academics go. The Italian Association of Canadian Studies, for example, might meet in Sicily and attract 200 or more academics from Italy, the Low Countries, France, and a few guests from Canadian universities. The general mood at such gatherings is serious and intelligent, but there is a certain puzzlement afoot. Why is it that the Canadian Studies specialists, those actively involved in the Association of Canadian Studies, are so rarely the scholars that the Italian specialists want to see? The Italians can read the books and articles, they can recognize the names of the people doing important work, and they can recognize that those are not the people involved in the Association.

In other words, the good Italian or Japanese scholar interested in Canadian subjects wants a chance to meet with and talk to the Canadian experts in his field, and only rarely are those experts part of the Association of Canadian Studies. What has occurred inevitably is that the Association has effectively taken control of the study of Canada abroad, and in the process it has intentionally or otherwise blocked the true transfer of ideas and knowledge. This cannot last much longer, for the good scholars abroad are far from being fools and they have already figured out what is happening. The same thing, however, cannot be said of the Departments of the Secretary of State and External Affairs in Ottawa, the sources of all funding.

It was the federal government that pushed Canadian Studies abroad, putting up the money for travel grants, for donations of books to university libraries, for the commissioning of books on Canada (the one produced in the United States, *Understanding Canada*, is an expensive scandal both for its costs and its contents), and for grants to the Canadian Studies associations abroad. All of this was essential if Canadian Studies was to develop abroad, and the result has not been entirely useless. There are good scholars in the U.S. and overseas working on Canadian topics, and a few years ago there were none. Some of the researchers come to Canada to dig through the archives for material on Italian fascism here in the 1930s or to track down poets or to study the Canadian educational system. That kind of scholarship deserves encouragement, and those researchers deserve every bit of assistance this country can offer them.

But, as in Canada, a number of individuals and institutions have simply fastened on to the Great Milch Cow that is the Canadian public purse. Fourth-rate universities in the United States that might have listed an obscure course on Canadian Indians in the past suddenly realized that this made them eligible to get all the free books on Canada they could handle and made their enterprising faculty eligible for large grants. And all an individual professor had to do to get an all-expense paid trip to Canada was to ask at the Embassy, indicate that he was thinking of working in Canadian Studies, and put together a plausible itinerary of Canadian Studies centres across the Dominion.

This is bad enough in the universities. Recently, however, the Ontario government, not to be outdone by Ottawa, has created a summer program for high school teachers interested in teaching about Canada. The result is a scheme that brings teachers from Germany, Belgium, and the Netherlands to Toronto for a three-week "course" – and one that sends Ministry officials to Europe each summer looking for teachers to come over the following year. Have we all gone mad?

Very simply, Canada is a country that is of marginal interest to most Americans, Europeans, and Asians. There are specialists at the university level who will delve into our history or economy or literature and some may develop genuine expertise that can illuminate our understanding of ourselves. So far this has not happened, and no one should be surprised that the process of scholarship in this new area of study abroad is slow. But it is unrealistic in the extreme to expect high school teachers to mount courses on Canada in rural North Carolina or Bavaria, and it is equally unrealistic to expect every university in Western Europe and Japan to teach their students about the Durham Report, the National Energy Program, or the novels of Graeme Gibson.

What does make sense, rather than the scatter-gun approach that Ottawa and the Association of Canadian Studies has been promoting, is to select three or four institutions abroad, to give them enough funding to get the research materials and the instructors they need, and to let nature take its course. With luck one of those universities might develop into a first-rate school of Canadian Studies abroad. Any other course is financially profligate and intellectually dishonest – and needless to say, that is precisely the direction in which we are heading. Does anyone anywhere believe for one milli-second that if a new government summoned the courage to cut off the funding of the Canadian Studies blossom abroad that the whole extra-Canadian empire would not wither and die?

Dollars Down the Tube

Unfortunately, that is unlikely to occur, for Canadian Studies is a motherhood buzzword in Ottawa. In 1978, as a "practical response" to the Symons Commission, the Secretary of State produced more than $1.5 million to promote Canadian Studies. Among other grants, $500,000 went to the Canada Studies Foundation to produce and publish materials for the public and high schools, a useful service to be sure but one that could have been accomplished just as well through the commercial publishing houses. The Association of Canadian Studies received $120,000 "to organize workshops and national conferences, prepare a publication program based on a series of Canadian biographies and inform Canadian studies faculty and students about conferences and financial assistance."[8] As a result, the Association of Canadian Studies, a small and scholastically undistinguished association, is virtually alone among Canadian learned societies in being able to have a full-time office staff. The biographies series is no doubt useful, but again this was something that could readily have been accomplished in the normal course of events. The money spent so far is relatively small in sum, particularly when compared with the billions poured into Canadair or the hundreds of millions squandered by Liberal MPs on patronage boondoggles. But waste is waste wherever it is to be found.

There was more to come. In 1983, Ottawa announced a series of writing, teaching, and research prizes in Canadian Studies[9] and, not to be outdone, Northern Telecom Ltd. funded a major award – $10,000 and a gold medal – to go to "an individual who has made an outstanding contribution to the development of Canadian studies." Again, that is a worthy aim, but more good candidates could have been found if the prize was for distinguished work in Canadian literature, sociology, or political science.

What is going on here is that both Ottawa and Northern Telecom are making the same mistake. Canadian Studies to them means the study of Canada; but to those running the Association of Canadian Studies and to those in charge of the funding in Ottawa, Canadian Studies means the discipline of Canadian Studies as it is practised in Canada and abroad by those who are not adherents to the traditional disciplines. Canadian Studies – and the money attached to it – belongs to those who seek not truth, as Bissell put it, but the holy grail.

Of course, the academics in the disciplines largely opted out of Canadian Studies once they saw the direction in which it was heading. It is just sour grapes to complain because support is going to an area in which one chose not to play. But if that area is in the hands of the mediocre? And if it is public funds that are being poured down the rathole? President Nixon was supposed to have named a third-rate jurist to the Supreme Court on the grounds that even the mediocre deserved representation. Congress refused to agree to that nomination; in Canada, however, there is no one to say nay.

What should be done, we believe, is to encourage not Canadian Studies but the study of Canada. In our view that can best be accomplished by supporting the first-class researchers who are now at work in Canadian sociology, politics, economics, history, and literature. Their research funding, as we suggested in Chapter VI, should come through the existing granting agencies and should be based on rigorous peer evaluation. That is not the case with the Secretary of State's grants for

Canadian Studies, where complaints about patronage are already being heard. Of course, the universities will not object if the federal or provincial governments and private business cough up funds for another Canadian Studies Centre; in their perilous financial condition any money is good money. But it would serve scholarship and the study of Canada far better if the universities said that their economics departments were doing first-class work of national importance and deserved support much more than their Canadian Studies people, if such is the truth. And the truth is that in every university in Canada those who study Canada do so with far more effect than those who work in Canadian Studies. Someday that may not be so, but it is now. It is time to call a halt to the waste of public and private funds in support of a quasi-discipline; it is time to urge the government to put its money were it can get scholarly results, and not merely the kudos that come from those who do not know what is happening.

Notes

1 *Canadian Historical Association Newsletter* (Winter, 1977).

2 Robert Page in *University Affairs* (December, 1972).

3 "The Recovery of a Canadian Tradition in Higher Education," *Canadian Journal of Higher Education*, VII (1977), p. 3.

4 *University Affairs* (November, 1981), p. 11.

5 Bissell, p. 3.

6 *University Affairs* (November, 1981), p. 11.

7 *Canadian Historical Review*, LXI (March, 1980), p. 118.

8 *University Affairs* (January, 1979).

9 In April 1984, the government provided $11.7 million more for Canadian Studies. One project apparently is to be a comic-book history of Canada for supermarket sale!

CHAPTER VIII
What Is To Be Done?

Picture Canada without universities. It is unthinkable. No modern society can function without universities, which are the essential capstones to the entire educational system. There is no real danger that Canadian universities will disappear because of mismanagement or government negligence and no reason why they should disappear because of the bad decisions made in recent years about admissions standards, curriculum, or unionization. And yet Canada's universities are sliding ever more deeply into mediocrity, and that is dangerous enough.

The greatest resource of any nation is the talent and energy of its people. Our educational system, from pre-school to graduate school, has been built slowly over hundreds of years of trial and error. We have introduced compulsory, free education through high school, paid for out of everyone's taxes, because we have come to accept the principle that an educated people is an essential national asset, lies at the foundation of our political and social well-being, and adds immeasurably to our national wealth. No one will argue with this today.

Universities are an integral part of that system even though attendance at university is not, and can never be, compulsory, and tuition is not free. But the same principles that should prompt Canadians to fight to maintain the existing system of elementary and secondary school education should lead, as well, into a struggle to re-establish a high-quality university system. If Canadian industry is to compete with the Americans, the Japanese, and the Koreans, we have to restore our universities. We need the engineers and scientists, the computer specialists, and the geologists, and we need the humanists, too, to ensure that we do not slip mindlessly into a technocratic state. The university graduates of today will also be the doctors, teachers, lawyers, and business and government leaders of tomorrow. And although universities are not, and should not be, for everyone, it is in the direct interests of all Canadians that young men and women of high intellectual ability alone should attend and should receive the best education possible. This has not been happening in recent years. The quality of the education offered in Canadian universities has eroded, particularly at the crucial undergraduate level where the basic B.A. and B.Sc. degrees are offered.

The problem began to develop in the early 1960s when rapid growth of university enrolments caused by the post-World War Two baby boom and the changing nature of university funding made universities slaves, willing slaves, alas, of governments. Direct government grants allowed, even forced, universities to expand too rapidly and to become too dependent on those grants with little independent income of their own. That had many drastic consequences. It increased the influence and interference of politicians in higher education with the result that too many universities now exist in this country, many in small communities that should be served only by community or junior colleges. Politicians used universities as they once used blacktop roads – to create local jobs – and they held out the hope to every voter that his or her children would be able to attend a university almost down the block. The result? A widespread duplication of services, a tremendous waste of money, a number of small universities across the country that should never have been built but which may never be closed down.

Political interference, sometimes as subtle persuasion, sometimes as direct pressure, has also had an impact on programs and quality. The politicians wanted more voters' children to go to university; the universities lowered entrance standards. The politicians wanted more "visible" results from the money they were pouring into universities, more "bang for the buck"; the universities stressed the vocational training part of higher education and de-emphasized the task that must lay at the very core of university – teaching people how to think.

The funding formulas that tied universities ever more closely to governments were destructive in themselves. In good years, when many students enrolled, there would be rivers of dollars. But if enrolments dropped suddenly, as they did in the early 1970s, the rivers dried to a trickle. Universities, like other large public institutions, cannot function with feast-or-famine budgeting. Programs and services, from grasscutting to student counselling, were cut back as faculty salaries fell and faculty and student morale plummeted. But in this annual lottery for students the universities were playing in a no-win game. When unemployment rose across the country at the start of this decade, so, too, did university enrolment. Many high school graduates decided to try their luck at university rather than on the job market, but government funding did not rise to keep pace. This was the era of savage cutbacks in all areas of government spending and universities have not been spared. So they are now bursting at the seams without enough money to carry on properly.

Finances have been at the root of many evils even inside universities. The division of many faculties of arts and sciences into two or even three new faculties has created watertight divisions between disciplines and between budgeting units. This means that several faculties now grab for dollars from the same pool of funds that once slaked the thirst of one. The rivalries prompt them to create programs that will discourage students from taking courses outside the faculty. This isolates students, leads to over-specialization, and places major obstacles in the path of real learning. Students are discouraged from looking outside their own area of specialization to take courses or programs that may be necessary for their intellectual development though not for the faculty-established guidelines. And the same problem continues at the department level and has led to the creation of over-specialized honours programs.

While universities were allowing themselves to get sucked closer to the maw of government, they also allowed their internal structures to evolve in ways that give control over universities to the wrong persons and which make internal reform very difficult. Boards have become business-dominated and their thinking too often reflects the mentality of the corporate boardroom when grappling with faculty and student affairs. An appalling number of university senates are dominated by administrators and students with faculty representatives in the minority. And many of those faculty representatives, elected from within individual faculties, sit because they are popular, not because they are excellent or demand high standards in admissions, grading, and programs. Faculty at most Canadian universities rushed, almost overnight, into trade unionism, creating great rigidities in board-faculty relations and enhancing the "we-they" atmosphere within the walls of academe. Although this has enhanced faculty power in some areas, it has defined that power and circumscribed it because of rules and regulations imposed by labour relations boards. Such a system favours the mediocre majority; it does not stimulate the exceptional and in some cases it works against them. Merit pay is now increasingly rare and at some universities tenure and promotion decisions can be imposed by arbitrators after long grievance procedures. A factory mentality is taking hold.

The most dramatic and perhaps most visible failure of universities has been in the area of admissions, grading, and curriculum. Entrance standards have been lowered to the point where almost every high school graduate is eligible to enter university at a time when it is clear that high school grades themselves are inflated. Too many incompetent students are being educated at the taxpayer's expense, and there is not enough money to provide scholarships and other means of financial support to good students who should be attending university regardless of their ability to pay. And once students enter university their grades today are likely to be higher than grades that would have been awarded ten or twenty years ago because of a creeping but very real grade inflation. There is too little control of grading and too little standardization of marks by the universities themselves. No one wanted to alienate students. If a department or faculty lost students, it lost funding as well and this created pressure to give grades away. When combined with the "good buddy" atmosphere that has developed in certain undergraduate disciplines, high grade point averages resulted.

Students are graduating with higher averages but

this certainly does not mean that they are better educated than their counterparts of two decades ago. The supermarket curriculum that exists for first-year university students at almost every campus in this country allows the ignorant to chart their own course. The core curriculum has disappeared. Students are no longer forced to take a course program that determines, in advance, how they will be introduced to the basic knowledge that lies at the foundation of a civilized society. They are allowed to take virtually whatever interests them, and they are allowed to take these courses in first year, where freedom of choice may well do the most damage, not the least. Honours programs have been devised that have become virtual routes to specialized ignorance. These extremely rigid programs ensure that a student will stay on a specialized path and will have little opportunity to learn in other important areas even though those areas may be closely related. At one time such graduates would have been called deficient; now they are called specialized.

This stemmed partly from the freedom demanded by students in the student revolt days of the 1960s, and partly as an inevitable outcome of the budgeting process within universities. But it is also a result of the influence students now wield on university senates and committees and even in the classroom through their evaluations of professors. This has given the novitiates a great deal of power in running the monastery and it is akin to giving high school or elementary school students a say in running their institutions.

If students have too large a say in what happens at universities, faculty, too, must share responsibility for becoming complacent about their institutions and about their role in higher education. And why not? They have the most complete job security system ever devised – tenure. There is no doubt that some means of protecting the free expression of ideas in a university is necessary, and tenure was created primarily to serve this purpose. But the price has been high, too high. Once granted tenure, after a probation period that can be as long as five years for junior staff but as short as nothing for senior academics who may be appointed with immediate tenure, they can hold their jobs for life whether or not they teach well, do research and publish, or serve the university community in some capacity. This is intolerable. And even though the faculty associations claim that this is not so, that procedures exist to dismiss tenured people that do nothing, this is, in reality, very difficult to do. The universities and the Canadian Association of University Teachers, together with local faculty associations, have created procedures for dismissal for cause that are so long, so drawn out, so complicated, and so expensive that most administrators (who want to keep things running smoothly, like administrators everywhere) would rather do nothing. So taxpayers' dollars are wasted, students are taught (or not taught in some cases) by people who are incompetent, and bright young graduates who should get a chance at these jobs are shut out. Those who are terminally lazy are protected along with those who take their responsibilities seriously. This is certainly no way to promote excellence. Nor is the virtually automatic granting of sabbaticals to almost anyone who holds tenure. Some professors work harder on sabbatical than they do during their years at teaching, but for others sabbaticals are nothing but long vacations at the expense of the universities. This must stop. Universities can surely judge from the track record who is entitled to sabbatical leave and who is not.

One good way to judge is by weighing the quality of research as measured by publication. "Publish or Perish" is a good thing, and it is time to get back to it with one proviso – the quality of the publication must be evaluated on a regular basis. There is too little publishing going on at Canadian universities although some disciplines are more guilty of this than others. Moreover, much that is published is junk. It is unreadable to most normal people, it is unoriginal, it is uninspiring, and it is a waste of good paper and ink. Universities tend to count and encourage tonnage rather than quality. There is, at the same time, a growing and extremely disturbing tendency of government agencies to try to direct research in the humanities and social sciences by deciding what "strategic" areas will receive the most funding. This will, if it continues, put the independent researcher at a distinct disadvantage and discourage Canadians from studying fields that the government does not deem "important." It will add to our ignorance and force us to rely on scholars from abroad.

University presses, essential for the dissemination of publication, are in poor shape in Canada and, by all indications, hanging on by the skin of their teeth. If they are not saved, vital avenues for the distribution of the fruits of research will disappear. Commercial publishers will not attempt to produce books that have potentially small reading audiences even though those audiences may be highly influential. They are, understandably, in the business of making a profit. But the limited-run books produced by many scholars must be published or the students of tomorrow will rely increasingly on research that is older and outdated, and this, too, will diminish the quality of higher education in Canada.

Students are learning more about Canada today than they were twenty years ago. This is a good thing. Some of what they are learning, however, particularly in Canadian Studies programs aimed at undergraduates, is not worth learning and millions of dollars are being squandered by a variety of agencies, associations, and government departments on "Canadian Studies" and on other "studies" programs such as native studies, northern studies, women's studies, and so on. Students in Canada must learn about Canada, from courses in Canadian history, Canadian sociology, Canadian geography, Canadian literature. The same applies to the North, to native people and other minorities, and to women. The cross-disciplinary mush being spooned out in "studies" programs gives students an extremely generalized knowledge about one subject with virtually no depth. At the same time, grants, prizes, journals, conferences, programs for study abroad, and programs for bringing foreigners to Canada have become a multimillion dollar industry that spins its wheels at best and accomplishes nothing at worst in advancing the knowledge Canadians have of their own country. It is not the Canadian Studies specialists who are telling us new things about Canada; it is the people who work in the traditional disciplines. There may well be a place for Canadian Studies *at the graduate level*, for students who have already had a solid grounding of knowledge in Canadian history or geography or any other of the traditional disciplines, but there is no room for it anywhere else. And surely the time has come for the taxpayers, for university administrators, and for faculty to question the squandering of "seed" money abroad that is usually little more than a bribe to entice foreign scholars to study "The Elephant and the Canadian Question" in a bid to climb aboard Ottawa's gravy train. There is no doubt that some serious foreign scholars, in traditional disciplines, are interested in Canada and do good work. They can still be encouraged, but in more traditional ways. But most of the money now spent abroad is much better spent in Canada.

The above constitutes a long, sad list of problems. It is not complete. We have not examined the difficulties in graduate and professional schools, and we have ignored other difficulties in the area of undergraduate education. We know there are problems there as well – a high percentage of professors at Canadian business schools and law schools do virtually no research and publishing and are better paid for it than their counterparts in other areas – but we have tried to point to the major areas of concern. We would be less than responsible, however (although many will accuse us of gross irresponsibility anyway), if we did not offer realistic solutions that can at least start the universities up the path to reform, rebuilding, and rejuvenation.

The process has to start at the roots, with funding. New methods of funding have to be devised that free universities from enrolment-driven financing and protect them from inflation at the same time. But this will not solve the entire problem. If governments have made the decision that they are about to reverse the universal access policies they were largely responsible for in the first place, they must have the courage to tell this to the electorate and to the universities and help set out the limits to student enrolment (while allowing universities the complete freedom to set higher admission standards). They must also help with the transition because universities will be undermined, and some will be virtually destroyed, if forced to fend for themselves. A process of rationalization must be started that will give students, faculty, and the public time, and the resources, to cope with the change.

Within the universities, a more rational way of distributing dollars should be worked out that will puncture the existing watertight compartments and discourage the designing of student programs that are too highly specialized. At the same time student fees at Canadian universities, which are very low compared to fees in the United States, must be raised to an average of $2,000 per student for a full year of undergraduate education. This will make more money available and allow the universities more freedom from government dollars than they now have, although they will continue to rely heavily on government financing for years to come. In addition, the public must insist, and the universities must lead the drive, that no student who can meet the new and higher entrance requirements of a university will be turned away because of inability to pay. That means scholarships and lots of them for the new meritocratic world.

Universities must raise their entrance standards. There are different ways of doing this, but it must be done. Entrance examinations devised by the universities would help students whose grades in high school were low but who truly have the ability to do university work. Those who have been bored by high school should not be shut out of university. There must be a way to allow the "late bloomers" in. It is also true, however, that even late bloomers may bloom too late and should not gain entrance. At some point in the life of every young person, he or she must become aware of life's realities and begin to shoulder the responsibility and bear the consequences of his or her own actions.

Once into university, students should be required to study a core curriculum, regardless of the direction they will eventually take. Honours programs should be rendered less rigid although the grade requirements for an honours degree must be maintained. University-wide committees should review grading procedures throughout the university each year to guard against grade inflation. An individual professor should have freedom to determine how grades will be apportioned in the classroom, but the university has the responsibility to see that *standards* are applied and that B and A grades are not handed out with complete abandon. Universities must also stop using students as an important part of the process of evaluating teachers. Evaluation of teaching performance should be done by peers who know what good teaching is and who can separate good teaching from mere entertainment.

The structure of the universities needs to be changed. Boards are too dominated by businessmen. Board members and administrators in universities should be rotated on a regular basis. Faculty members should be given an absolute majority on senates and full professors should have the power to appoint a part of their number to some of those faculty positions. Students should be removed from senates and the number of administrators, especially those with votes, should be reduced to a bare minimum. It is time, in other words, to put the academic affairs of the university back where they belong, in the hands of the professors, and to try to ensure that at least some of those professors are among the very best in the institution. Administrators should have little or no say in promotion decisions. These decisions must be made by the best scholars in each institution.

It will be very difficult to reverse the trend to trade unionism, but, as we have written, it is a trend fraught with danger. Universities and their faculty associations should turn back to the shared-authority approach first recommended by Duff and Berdahl but with built-in systems to resolve disputes over salary and fringe benefits that will inevitably arise between boards and faculty. Items that can be grieved should be limited to those covered in the system for resolving salary disputes. Tenure (in those universities where it may survive) and promotion must not be placed within the reach of arbitrators.

Tenure itself must be eliminated. As it now exists it has become blanket job security. Professors should be free to express themselves; they must not be free to be lazy. A system of five-year renewable contracts should be substituted for tenure. In each case, a *person* should be up for review every five years, not a *position*. In this way there will be no danger that good people will be dismissed for budgetary reasons in the process. The five-year review should be conducted by peers, not administrators, drawn from across the university with representation from the faculty association. Such a system will create new incentive to faculty to perform the duties for which they have been hired. This may not be as strong a protection of academic freedom as tenure, but it will do far more to stimulate excellence. Such peer review committees should be instructed to weigh quality, not quantity, in a professor's output of research and publishing, quality as measured by national and international standards. No potential Einstein should be dismissed because he did not turn out "enough." Those who cannot or will not publish, but whose teaching abilities are clearly high, should not be dismissed but directed to teach more than those who do publish. In this way their special talents would be put to greater use and there would be less of a teaching load on those who do vast amounts of research and publication.

Some of the millions that governments are now throwing away on "studies" programs should be directed toward the university presses of this country so that they can be nursed back to health. And university presses should be encouraged to find better ways of marketing books that might prove more attractive to a Canadian public that grows larger and better educated every year.

All of these suggestions, if instituted, would begin the

process of reform. Higher education in Canada has to be restored to health. There are too many vested interests in the present system to expect much reform from within it. It is only when the public finally decides to put a stop to The Great Brain Robbery that rehabilitation can begin. Let *something* be done, quickly!